Y0-CBM-686

EDUCATION

HIGHER EDUCATION
IN A
CHANGING ECONOMY

HIGHER EDUCATION IN A CHANGING ECONOMY

Edited by

KATHARINE H. HANSON
JOEL W. MEYERSON

American Council on Education ⋈ *Macmillan Publishing Company*
NEW YORK
Collier Macmillan Canada
TORONTO
Maxwell Macmillan International
NEW YORK   OXFORD   SINGAPORE   SYDNEY

Macmillan Publishing Company
866 Third Avenue, New York, N.Y. 10022

Collier Macmillan Canada, Inc.
1200 Eglinton Avenue East, Suite 200
Don Mills, Ontario M3C 3N1

Library of Congress Catalog Card Number: 90-38752

Printed in the United States of America

printing number
1 2 3 4 5 6 7 8 9 10

Library of Congress Cataloging-in-Publication Data

Higher education in a changing economy / edited by Katharine H.
Hanson, Joel W. Meyerson.
    p.   cm.—(American Council on Education/Macmillan series on
higher education)
    Includes bibliographical references and index.
    ISBN 0-02-897201-5
    1. Education, Higher—Economic aspects—United States.
I. Hanson, Katharine.   II. Meyerson, Joel W.
III. American Council on Education.   IV. Series: American Council on
Education/Macmillan series on higher education.
LC67.62.H54   1990
338.4'737873—dc20   90-38752
                                                              CIP

CONTENTS

FOREWORD

In reflecting on how to introduce a discussion of higher education in a changing economy, I was struck by how incomprehensible this subject would have seemed at an earlier time indeed, throughout almost all the history of higher education in this country. It probably wasn't that changes in the economy were actually irrelevant to universities; I do not suppose that the modern university could have emerged in this country without the industrial revolution. Certainly, the airplane, the telephone, the television, and the computer all made enormous differences, for better or for worse, in the way universities conduct their business and in the way research is carried on. But as I read the history of higher education, there wasn't a great deal of awareness of those changes. There was a much greater sense of being protected and removed from society. Even business cycles left universities relatively unscathed, a protection that kept them from thinking a great deal about the effects of the economy. Their endowments were so small that stock market fluctuations were not of immediate moment. Government outlays did not amount to very much. Only a few hundred thousand dollars were paid by the federal government for research purposes up to World War II. Depressions had caused various difficulties but also curtailed the costs that universities faced. So, it was well into the postwar period that changes began to take place—like recessions accompanied by higher prices—that made universities acutely aware of the economy.

Now of course we are vulnerable on almost every point to what goes on in the economy. Our endowments are subject to fluctuations in the stock market. Our research is affected by government policies that are, in turn, affected by the economy. We feel the effects of international economic events—the costs that go up when OPEC is powerful and down when it is not. Our gifts are affected by prosperity, and so it goes.

The other side of the equation is the contribution that universities make to the economy as well as their vulnerability to it. That has always struck me as a much more imponderable issue. I am sometimes troubled to note that the U.S. economy did best relative to other countries when our universities were mediocre. Particularly in terms of productivity, our relative performance has been rather appalling during the period in which our economists won almost all the Nobel prizes and our scientists led the world. But I am sure that is an aberration that will be explained in the course of time. We know that in the long run, economic vitality must depend on three important ingredients: expert knowledge, new discoveries, and highly trained personnel. For better or worse, universities are the primary source of at least two of those ingredients and an important source of the third. Somehow, therefore, we must be important.

However incomprehensible or irrelevant our topic would have seemed for most of the history of higher education in this country, it has certainly become extremely important today. The three essays presented here are by experts on the financing of higher education. The commentaries following them are all by individuals deeply concerned with and involved in colleges and universities, and the impact of the economy on them. Collectively, these writings should increase our understanding of what the future may hold for higher education in the United States.

Derek Bok

CONTRIBUTORS

Derek Bok is President of Harvard University.

Richard Eckaus is Ford International Professor of Economics at Massachusetts Institute of Technology.

Bruce Johnstone is Chancellor of the State University of New York.

Stephen Lewis, Jr. is President of Carleton College.

Lawrence Lindsay is Associate Professor of Economics at Harvard University. He is currently Special Assistant to the President for Policy Development.

William Massy is Vice President for Business and Finance of Stanford University.

Harold Shapiro is President of Princeton University.

Richard Spies is Financial Vice President of Princeton University.

INTRODUCTION

The American economy is changing, and the changes will affect higher education as never before. This was the message economists and educators brought to a special symposium sponsored by the Consortium on Financing Higher Education (COFHE) and Coopers & Lybrand (C&L). The papers presented by three distinguished economists at the symposium and the discussions which followed form the core of this book.

WHY IS THIS SUBJECT IMPORTANT NOW?

America's more than three thousand colleges and universities hold a preeminent position in the world. In spite of sometimes dire predictions of decline, the overall industry of higher education has succeeded. So why did COFHE and C&L hold a special symposium now? Should American educators worry about the future? First, let's briefly look back and see how we got to this point.

Higher education has prospered since World War II. Total enrollment increased more than fourfold between the 1949–50 and 1979–80 school years, while total enrollment per institution almost tripled during the same period. In spite of a demographic downturn in the college-age population, America's colleges and universities increased in numbers and in total enrollment during the last decade. However, troubling signs haunt higher education as it enters the 1990s:

- Annual increases in the Higher Education Price Index (HEPI) which have exceeded annual increases in the Consumer Price Index (CPI) since 1982.
- A shift in current fund revenue sources from predominantly government funding in the 1970s to more volatile internal and private funding in the 1980s.
- The sometimes questionable readiness of entering American freshmen, who for instance, in an analysis of international mathematics testing for advanced twelfth-grade mathematics students, ranked next to last among 13 participating nations.
- A change in output—the number of master's and doctoral degrees awarded to foreign students increased 55 percent and 42 percent,

respectively, between the mid-1970s and mid-1980s, while the number of these degrees awarded to U.S. students actually declined during the same period.

- The increase in questions and criticism by the public and political leaders about the quality and value of the education provided by America's colleges and universities.

Higher education's success to date is at least partially attributable to a healthy U.S. economy, which has enjoyed a postwar period of overall unprecedented growth and prosperity. Real GNP in 1972 dollars increased almost threefold between 1950 and 1980, while real GNP per capita almost doubled during the same period. Although some economists had predicted a marked decline, the U.S. economy sailed through the 1980s relatively unscathed, with only regional and sectoral causes for concern. But worrisome signs continue to cloud the national economic horizon as the United States approaches a new decade. These include the following:

- A downward trend in the GNP rate of growth since the 1970s
- A trade deficit since 1982 after 85 years of nearly continuous trade surpluses
- A persistent federal budget deficit in the billions of dollars since 1974
- Wall Street's "Black Monday,"about which investment banker Felix Rohatyn has said, "We came within half an hour of really blowing up the Western economic system."

The economic consequences of the federal and international deficits combined with the low GNP growth rate are not clear, even to experts. Optimistic analysts observe recent improvements in budget and trade deficits and conclude prospects for future growth are good. Middle-of-the-road economists say the United States can get along with a low growth rate as long as the twin deficits don't escalate further. Pessimists point to the persistence and size of the budget and trade shortfalls as major obstacles to future growth and as signals of structural weakness in the U.S. economy.

Although experts disagree on the meaning of specific events, most agree the American economy will change in response to twin deficits, low growth, and a volatile market; and the changes will clearly have an impact on the financial health of America's colleges and universities. To understand better the relationship between the macroeconomy and higher education and to begin preparing for the changes, COFHE and C&L invited economists and educators to the special symposium.

SYMPOSIUM PARTICIPANTS

Lawrence B. Lindsey, Associate Professor of Economics at Harvard University and Faculty Research Fellow at the National Bureau of Economic Research, took the most optimistic view of the national economy. Espousing "supply-side economics," Lindsey characterized economic change as the reemergence of economic individualism and the university as the beneficiary of the new trend. Richard S. Eckaus, Ford International Professor of Economics at the Massachusetts Institute of Technology, took a more middle-of-the-road approach. He described the current U.S. economy, prospects for its future economic growth, and the specific implications for higher education. Harold T. Shapiro, President of Princeton University and Professor of Economics, spoke of the economic impact of recent scholarly and technological developments and the capacity of colleges and universities to accommodate these changes within the existing institutional framework.

Four panelists moderated by Derek Bok, President of Harvard University, led a discussion of the themes which emerged from the presentations. The panelists were:

- Bruce Johnstone, Chancellor of the State University of New York.
- Stephen R. Lewis, Jr., President of Carleton College.
- William F. Massy, Vice President for Business and Finance of Stanford University
- Richard R. Spies, Financial Vice President of Princeton University

Brief summaries of the three papers given at the symposium and the ensuing panel discussion are presented below.

THE UNIVERSITY AND THE REEMERGENCE OF ECONOMIC INDIVIDUALISM
LAWRENCE B. LINDSEY

Throughout history, individualist and statist themes have alternately held prominence. The individualist view holds that society benefits when each individual is allowed to work in his or her own self-interest. Under the statist or collectivist theme, the definition of well-being is set by society instead of by the individual. Lindsey points to the numerous free-market economies that are flourishing while their socialist neighbors struggle as evidence that individualist-based economics are currently ascendant throughout the world. These economies are more adaptable to change, and therein lies their success, according to Lindsey. Such an economy also creates opportunities for higher education.

When decision-making power devolves to individuals, the creativity and thought processes taught by a liberal arts curriculum become especially valuable.

The current condition of the U.S. economy was Lindsey's second major topic. With roughly one-third of the nation's output currently channeled through federal, state, and local coffers, the government may have reached its fiscal limit. Although American industry has restructured and become more competitive during the last five years, foreign investment in the United States—used largely to finance the federal budget deficit—has surpassed outflows of capital and goods to international markets. Government-run central banks have been the principal lenders since 1986, instead of profit-seeking foreign individuals with confidence in the U.S. economy. This recent development signals the inappropriateness of continued borrowing. The United States has three options—higher interest rates, a further devalued dollar, or less borrowing—and will probably adopt a combination of all three.

According to Lindsey, the federal budget deficit is a large but not insurmountable problem. It could be eliminated in four or five years by simply restraining spending growth to the rate of inflation (about 4 percent per year). Although a higher tax rate is an unlikely alternative so soon after the 1986 Tax Reform Act, bringing currently untaxed activities into the tax base would increase revenues without raising rates. For instance, taxing the investment and auxiliary services income of colleges and universities could broaden the tax base in two ways, according to a recent Ways and Means Committee study.

Lindsey proposes changing the status of colleges and universities to that of taxable corporations. Under this method, profits from endowment income or auxiliary services would partially offset losses from education, but would rarely result in taxable income.

At best, in the foreseeable future federal expenditures for higher education will keep pace with inflation, according to Lindsey. Colleges and universities will have to look to customers—students—to make up the difference. The institutions that will survive and prosper are those that can best satisfy the market demands of their customers.

THE U.S. ECONOMY AND HIGHER EDUCATION
RICHARD S. ECKAUS

According to Richard Eckaus, the U.S. economy appears strong on the surface, but signs of decline lurk under the aggregate numbers. The monetary and fiscal policies of the 1980s generated federal and trade deficits, each of which exceeded $150 billion by 1986. Only in 1986 did median family income equal levels previously achieved in the early 1970s; median individual income has not recovered to its 1973 high. Furthermore, uneven sectoral and regional economic performance has created painful dislocations in some areas. Analysts worry that the United States is losing its competitive edge, but studies on this question are inconclusive.

In spite of these problems, Eckaus surmises that the U.S. economy is capable of sustaining substantial growth rates if more productive resources—natural resources, capital, and labor—are used with greater productivity. However, the capital resource presents some particularly thorny problems. Declining household savings rates combined with the substantial federal deficit, or dissavings, have greatly increased U.S. dependence on foreign savings during the 1980s. Economists present varying scenarios, ranging from optimistic to pessimistic, that may result from the low U.S. savings rates.

Clearly, the federal deficit is a significant constraint on future prospects for economic growth. The difficulty in reducing the deficit is compounded by lower tax revenues, resulting from the tax reduction act of 1981, and the increased proportion of federal monies needed for entitlement and other mandatory programs. Defense spending and interest payments increased sharply during the 1980s as well, and squeezed nondefense, discretionary items. Reducing the federal deficit involves various mixtures of lower spending, higher growth, and more taxes.

How will the deficit affect higher education? Although dollar amounts of federal assistance to higher education increased over the last ten years, the government's share of total revenues declined substantially, while private and internal sources of revenue made up the shortfall. Budgetary constraints necessitated by the deficit make future increases in federal assistance to higher education, including those for research, highly uncertain.

The changing American demography affects higher education's future as well. The number of white 18-year-olds in the U.S. population will decline approximately 16 percent by 1992, reducing demand for enrollment by higher education's primary customers. However, foreign students will fill some of the vacancies. Income is a key determinant of the participation rate in higher education. Women's participation in the U.S. labor force has pushed up family incomes, and enhanced families' ability to pay for college. World economic growth and a devalued dollar have enabled foreign students to pay U.S. tuition costs.

The U.S. economy influences the financial conditions of higher education although there is no model to suggest how institutions would behave under different economic scenarios. In the conventional marketplace, firms compete to maximize their profits. Similarly, Eckaus suggests, colleges and universities compete within their market groups (research universities or two-year colleges, for example) for superior students, prestigious faculty members, and research contracts and facilities. The institutions that are perceived to be of higher quality improve their access to funds from foundation endowments, alumni gifts, higher tuitions, and research contracts. Quality competition, as well as general inflation, increases higher education's costs. High costs would not become a problem if federal tuition assistance programs and the pool of qualified students able to pay high tuitions were large enough to accommodate all the institutions. Since this is not the case, the future favors less costly public institutions, especially at the undergraduate level. Eckaus further concludes that the evolution of national attitudes toward higher education will influence its future.

HIGHER EDUCATION IN A CHANGING ECONOMY: THE SCHOLARLY AND ECONOMIC IMPERATIVES
HAROLD T. SHAPIRO

Within the context of the macro- and microeconomic forces presented by Lindsey and Eckaus, Harold Shapiro directs his attention to the economic impact of scholarly and technological developments on higher education. Underlying his presentation is the question: Can higher education continue to combine teaching with a serious commitment to scholarship?

Current economic and scholarly trends strain higher education's role as a buffer against changing societal priorities and as a foundation for academic freedom. According to Shapiro, growing apprehension about the following issues is symptomatic of the tension:

- Chronic perceived funding shortages
- Public concern about the high cost and price of a college education
- Increasingly unpredictable flow of resources for education and scholarship
- Perceived inability of discipline-based scholars to work with colleagues and across disciplines
- Apparent rift between graduate and undergraduate education
- Difficulty bridging alternate viewpoints in the humanities and some of the social sciences
- Public anxiety about the nature of scientific research within the university and higher education's responsibility for students' ethical and moral development
- Selection procedures for an undergraduate curriculum
- Poor general literacy in science
- Failure of higher education to raise participation rates of minorities

Shapiro highlights several developments which underlie the above apprehensions. Advances in scientific, computer, and communication technologies demand greater investments of capital per faculty member and student. These growing capital needs necessitate the setting of internal funding priorities and the reliance on relatively unpredictable external research funds. They also change the scholarly environment. The study of increasingly complex systems requires larger support staffs and more interdisciplinary research among scholars.

Other concerns for higher education include increasing demand for student support services, the end of mandatory retirement policies for faculty, high cost of government regulations, projected shortages of scholars and salary requirements for certain disciplines, the crisis in the American elementary and high school educational system, and the shorter time frame between development of new ideas and marketable products.

Shapiro concurs that prospects for increased federal funding are limited. Although the industry cannot influence the economy's future direction, he suggests that institutions can become more productive and consider greater specialization in response to rising costs.

PANEL DISCUSSION
DEREK BOK, PRESIDENT OF HARVARD UNIVERSITY

Derek Bok put the symposium topic of higher education in a changing economy in historical perspective. Although higher education was never totally insulated from shifts in the national economy, it was more removed from society until the postwar period. U.S. colleges and universities have become increasingly vulnerable to the changing economy on almost every point since World War II. On the other hand, the nation's economic vitality depends on the expert knowledge, new discoveries, and skilled labor force that higher education produces.

Bok concurred with all three presenters that the fiscal environment faced by colleges and universities will get tougher as government support wanes and as pressure to broaden the tax base increases. However, he warned that economic models do not take into account higher education's resiliency. Bok concluded that higher education can adapt to a tougher fiscal environment using the same resourcefulness the industry has demonstrated in the past.

BRUCE JOHNSTONE, CHANCELLOR OF THE STATE UNIVERSITY OF NEW YORK

Bruce Johnstone considered the following two questions in response to the issues raised by the three economists:

- Can the macroeconomy sustain higher education's increasing costs?

- Should the industry prepare for the macroeconomic forces or let the macroeconomy force changes in the microeconomics of our institutions?

As partial answers, Johnstone noted that higher education can be produced more cheaply by doing less for faculty—fewer resources for scholarship, such as equipment, support staff, computer and travel time—and for students—fewer facilities and amenities and less advising and tutoring. The industry could reduce the amount of time necessary to obtain a degree or increase overall faculty teaching loads. However, the enormous internal and societal resistance to such fundamental change makes it virtually impossible to plan significant cost reductions with these methods.

As Chancellor of the 64-campus SUNY system, Johnstone pointed out the particular constraints of public institutions which, in his opinion, feel the effects of the macroeconomy faster than private colleges. Public colleges and universities must address public demands for quality education in conjunction with taxpayer resistance to tuition increases, additional funding requests, and faculty and administrative salary increases.

STEPHEN LEWIS, JR., PRESIDENT OF CARLETON COLLEGE

Stephen Lewis raised several questions about the theme of higher education's rising costs:

- Who should pay? Parents? Government? Corporations? Foundations?
- Who should judge the output?
- What will happen to minority representation on the nation's college campuses if costs continue to rise?
- What should be the balance between research or scholarship and teaching?

Lewis pointed out that colleges and universities need to be concerned about industry-specific demographics as well as the interrelationships between higher education and the general economy. For instance, the projected large number of faculty retirements in the 1990s is one issue that will affect only the academic world. In other cases, higher education is affected by the general economy—the current pressure to make academic salaries competitive with those of private industry is just one example.

The economic meaning of student financial assistance is not clear. Tuition aid seems to be a discount from an arbitrary tuition price that covers only part of the cost. Moreover, institutions use tuition aid for different reasons. Strong institutions have large aid programs to diversify their student body, while weak institutions use financial aid as a further discount to increase the number of students in attendance.

According to Lewis, responses to the national economy need to be institution specific. Such responses require continual analysis and planning to understand better the micro- and macroeconomic forces that influence each institution's future.

WILLIAM MASSY, VICE PRESIDENT FOR BUSINESS AND FINANCE, STANFORD UNIVERSITY

According to William Massy, quality competition drives costs up, but there's little incentive to hold prices down given the low elasticity of demand. Enrollment has increased over the last several years in spite of the demographic downturn and high tuition costs. Private research universities are the price leaders. It's always been assumed that research subsidizes undergraduate education, but it may be the other way around. If this is the case, costs—followed by prices—would be driven up at research universities, and other price-following institutions would soon raise tuitions in response.

On the negative side, the future fiscal pressures from declining federal support and from potential taxes are causes of great concern to colleges and universities. But on the positive side, higher education is currently in a strong domestic and international market. Foreign students, largely financed by their parents or governments, contribute approximately $10 to $15 thousand each to the U.S. economic system for college tuition, room, and board. Domestic participation rates are trending up for the majority. The challenge for the 1990s will be how to use higher education's strong market position to move to a point of greater strength, to adapt to the market and yet continue to be a buffer against society.

In Massy's opinion, the macroeconomy looks solid, although a policy error could lead to major difficulties. Inflation, stagflation, and recession are still possibilities for which higher education needs to develop contingency plans. The big economic question is whether the rest of the world will continue to lend to the United States.

Colleges and universities are becoming more capital intensive, but it's increasingly difficult to raise the necessary funds due to a worldwide shortage of capital. The culture of higher education does not lend itself to reserving current revenue for transfers to plant. Rather, institutions of higher learning spend for the benefit of today's faculty and student. Massy supports the Financial Accounting Standards Board's (FASB's) recent position on asset depreciation for colleges and universities as a step in the right direction.

Massy concludes that the industry needs a workable theory of finance and expenditure to predict how colleges and universities will react to different economic scenarios.

RICHARD SPIES, FINANCIAL VICE PRESIDENT, PRINCETON UNIVERSITY

According to Richard Spies, colleges and universities are uniquely public/private institutions. In their private role, academic institutions compete fiercely for students, faculty, and funding. However, they are not profit maximizers as Adam Smith said organizations were. Examples of higher education's public behavior include the following:

- Subsidizes individual customers with tuition aid instead of using aid to increase the customer base
- Uses technology to make the product more complicated and expensive instead of to reduce labor costs
- Cost-shares on sponsored research to satisfy individual faculty members rather than an overall business plan and gives away the published results
- Sustains allegiance to liberal arts even though some customers want a more relevant product offering
- Takes pride in charging students only 60 percent of the cost and resorts to a complicated tithing system to make up the difference
- Lets students and employees advise the president

Spies argues that the current public/private environment works to the advantage of higher education and the public. Moreover, colleges and universities should not be too pessimistic about the future, but instead focus on bettering their individual institutions.

LOOKING AHEAD

Amid general agreement that the 1990s will be an era of increased competition for resources, participating economists and educators focused on the already rising cost trajectory of higher education. Serving the public in an increasingly expensive environment will be the coming challenge for America's colleges and universities. To help institutions meet this challenge and prepare for the future, Carol Frances has identified "key economic indicators for higher education." These indicators are presented in the Appendix to this book.

Katharine H. Hanson is Executive Director of the Consortium on Financing Higher Education.

Joel W. Meyerson is a partner of Coopers & Lybrand and director of C&L's higher education practice.

SECTION I
POSITIONS

1

THE UNIVERSITY AND THE REEMERGENCE OF ECONOMIC INDIVIDUALISM

LAWRENCE B. LINDSEY

For centuries the university has been widely considered to be separate from the society in which it operates. The term *ivory tower* has been used to characterize this separation, suggesting an unsullied environment above the problems and temptations of everyday life. Our institutions cultivate this image in a physical sense, often surrounding themselves with brick walls and wrought-iron gates.

Daily experience has taught us that the shelter offered by those walls is merely metaphorical. The troubles of the real world pour through our gates along with our students, faculty, and employees. Today, the university is not a refuge from change, but a focal point for all of the crosscurrents of society. We are in the midst of a major change in our economic, political, and social mores. In my view, this change is best characterized as the reemergence of economic individualism.

If our institutions make the proper strategic decisions now, these impending changes will leave higher education with an even more valuable role in the twenty-first century than it has today. However, adaptation to the new environment will not be easy. Those institutions that continue to adhere to the norms of the recent past will enter the next century at a serious handicap, and many will not survive.

The reemergence of economic individualism will produce dramatic changes in the way we operate. First, the reworking of the intellectual landscape regarding the role of the individual in society will greatly expand the demand for the kind of services universities offer. Decision-making power which used to be concentrated in bureaucratic and hierarchical organizations will increasingly devolve to individuals. This devolution of decision making will place a premium on education and creativity, and thus on the types of services which universities offer.

This increased demand for our services is the key to our long-term economic survival.

Second, the balance of economic power will begin to shift away from the state and toward the individual. This change has already begun. The fiscal situation we are now experiencing in America is symptomatic of the change in the balance of power between the state and the individual. These fiscal changes will compel those responsible for the financial health of our institutions to rethink the way we do business. We will no longer be able to rely on government for funding to the same extent as we do today. Instead, we will become more like other businesses, reliant on the goodwill of our consumers, both past and present.

Third, the economic changes which have made the reemergence of economic individualism possible will force us to change our internal operations. The successful university of the twenty-first century will offer a product different from its contemporary counterpart, one geared to the changing tastes of our customers. In particular, the current overwhelming stress on research output will shift increasingly toward a renewed emphasis on quality of teaching. The internal decisions necessary to meet this change in the tastes of our customers will be the ones with which most universities are likely to have the greatest difficulty.

THE REEMERGENCE OF ECONOMIC INDIVIDUALISM

Let us begin by considering what is meant by the term *economic individualism* and examining the evidence of its reemergence. The intellectual history of my profession has involved many changes in emphasis over the past several centuries. But two competing themes have persisted throughout: individualism on the one hand, and statism or collectivism on the other. The essence of economics has always been maximization subject to constraints, or more generically, making the most out of a given situation. What has been subject to debate is not this materialistic theme, but the objective to be maximized. What is it that we are to make the most of?

The individualist theme in economics is that economic actors, households, and firms know best what it is they want. If they are allowed to work in their own self-interest then each individual will be able to make himself or herself as well off as possible. In this context, social welfare is derived directly by aggregating the welfare of individuals.

The collectivist or statist theme holds that individual satisfaction is quite distinct from social welfare. We may, in the words of one of my Harvard colleagues, witness public poverty amidst an affluent society. In this statist construct of the world, collective goals are set, and the economic system is designed to attain these goals. While a certain level of individual well-being may be considered one of these goals, the definition of well-being is determined by society and not the individual. In this world view, the state is the logical tool for taking actions to maximize social well-being, with individual action relegated to a subservient role.

Neither the individualist nor the statist view has ever completely dominated the field of political economy. A brief review of history indicates that individualism and statism have alternated in their domination of thought. Early economic thinking and policy making was dominated by statist views and prescriptions. Machiavelli urged his Prince to control the currency and the courts and leave the rest to others. The potential debasement of the currency provided sufficient revenue-making power for the Prince to carry on his military adventures. This theme was more formally developed into the concept of mercantilism, which held that the welfare of the society was measured by the stock of bullion held by the state. This mercantilist view of the world held that foreign trade should be run in surplus in order to accumulate bullion, with state-sponsored protection of industry to accomplish that result. Analysis of mercantilism shows that the accumulation of bullion by the state entails a substantial sacrifice in individual well-being. Unfortunately, variations of this mercantilist theme are still common political currency. Protectionism is an important part of the demands of particular political constituencies. Invariably, mercantilism requires a transfer of economic power to the state from individuals.

The intellectual assault on statism began with Adam Smith's publication of *The Wealth of Nations* in 1776. But it was not until the middle of the nineteenth century that individualist economics, as expressed by David Ricardo, and later by John Stuart Mill and the Utilitarians, found a dominant role in policy making. The decision by Great Britain to adopt free trade and open market led to an explosion of living standards. This, combined with the international influence of Britain, made individualist economics the dominant mode of thought until after the First World War.

It took the Great Depression of the 1930s for statism again to dominate economic thought. The leading role of the state in setting economic priorities and the policies for attaining these goals became generally accepted. In the extreme, this statist economic philosophy found an ally in statist political philosophy as exhibited by communism and fascism. But it would be wrong to confuse statist economic views with statist political views. Even within democratic societies, the acceptable level of state economic power hit truly record levels. The share of national product controlled by these democratic states rose from less than 10 percent to a minimum of 30 percent and sometimes as high as 50 or 60 percent.

Heavy taxation, extensive government regulation, and an active government promotion of employment were all considered manifestations of this policy.

In America, the dominance of a statist-oriented economic philosophy never led to the extinction of either the individual nor the market. A view known as the Samuelsonian consensus emerged within the economics profession. Markets and individuals would continue to make most of the economic decisions, but subject to governmental constraints. Governments would play an active regulatory role in markets to produce desired outcomes. Individual initiative would be harnessed to a system of highly progressive taxation. The state's role was to manage actively the demand for goods and services. The dominant view was that with the tools at its disposal the government could engineer any desired distribution of income at any given level of unemployment consistent with any desired rate of inflation.

The intellectual assault on this statist economic philosophy began in the academic journals two or three decades ago. But only in the 1970s, with this philosophy in complete political dominance, did its failures become evident. It was clear that the results of state regulation were not arguably better than those of unfettered though admittedly imperfect markets. The highly progressive tax system was imposing obvious economic distortions without either significantly changing the distribution of income or eliminating poverty. Finally, the macroeconomic calamity of the late 1970s, with double-digit inflation and rising unemployment, made it clear that active state intervention could not even achieve the acceptable macroeconomic targets. What began as a slow academic chipping away at the philosophy of active state involvement became an intellectual and political rout. Today, the individualist economic principles are ascendant, though far from completely dominant, in both intellectual discourse and the formulation of policy.

The reemergence of individualist economic thought is nowhere near its end. As the above discussion indicates, the competing themes of economics develop over a period of time within academic thought and then emerge to dominate policy making. The period of dominance is not measured in years, but in decades. Therefore, it is a serious mistake to associate the current trend toward individualist and free-market economic thinking with a single political leader. The departure of Ronald Reagan from the political scene will not mean the end of what pundits call the Reagan Revolution. Although Reagan personifies individualist economic thinking, the mode of analysis did not begin with him and will not end with him. Even if a new administration should try to reverse course toward a more statist direction, it will ultimately be defeated by what have now become the new economic facts of life.

The triumph of individualist economic thinking is worldwide, and is based not merely on intellectual discussion, but also on the over-whelming weight of economic experience. The simple fact is that statist economics does a terrible job of delivering material well-being to its con-stituents and is virtually incapable of functioning in the context of rapid economic change. Even those societies in which statist thought is the official political creed are abandoning statist economic policies.

Events in Eastern Europe made this point clear throughout 1989. Economic desperation forced the Polish government to move toward the first free elections in Eastern Europe in more than 40 years. East Ger-mans flocked to the West when first given the opportunity. In nation after nation, the cult of the state proved to have nothing more behind it than the point of the bayonet. In China, which abandoned state con-trol of agriculture a decade ago with extraordinary results, the bayonet has made a tragic, but by all accounts temporary, comeback in 1989. Still, the collapse of some of the bastions of state power augers well for the reemergence of economic individualism.

In the third world the abandonment of statist economic models is quite profound. The success stories of economic development have been the so-called four dragons of east Asia: Hong Kong, Taiwan, Singapore, and South Korea. The success of South Korea, which was considered an economic basket case just 25 years ago, is particularly dramatic when contrasted with its statist neighbor to the north. Free-market Thailand is an economic success while neighboring socialist Burma struggles to feed itself. In Africa, capitalist Kenya has the fastest growing economy while next door, socialism in Tanzania has turned the continent's former breadbasket into a net importer of food.

In Europe, Margaret Thatcher has turned England from an eco-nomic laughingstock into an economic leader. Who would have thought ten years ago that Britain's economic growth rate would ever outpace that of Germany? Socialism was tried briefly in France by Mitterand and abandoned after two years of disastrous results. Europe as a whole is moving toward a free internal market in all goods and services by 1992.

In this country, a decisive move toward individualist economic poli-cies has literally turned the economy around. In the midst of the latest presidential campaign, critics were fond of pointing out that real family income in America is the same today as it was in 1973. This, they say, is proof that the country has just been spinning its wheels. What these critics fail to note is that economic performance since 1973 should really be viewed as two distinct periods. In the first half of this period, 1973 to 1981, median family income, adjusted for inflation, fell from $30,820 to $27,977, a decline of nearly 10 percent. Since then, the direction has been uphill, so that by 1987 we had reversed the decline of the 1970s and set a new record high of $30,853. In short, the period since 1973 was not one of stagnation, but rather exhibits a V-shape: sharp decline in the late 1970s, when statist-oriented economic policies predominated; an equally sharp improvement during the 1980s, when more individualist policies prevailed.

The litany of statistics on economic progress is impressive. We are in the midst of the longest peacetime economic expansion in history. A greater percentage of Americans is at work today than at any other time on record, including the midst of the Second World War. Inflation has been cut from 13 percent to just 4 percent. Family income has outpaced inflation for every identifiable group in the population: whites, blacks, Hispanics, and Asian-Americans, married couples, single-parent families, and single individuals living by themselves. Full-time wages for males have kept pace with inflation while part-time male earnings have increased faster than inflation. Female wages have not only grown faster than inflation, but much faster than male wages as well.

The reason that market-based, individualist economic policies work best is that they offer the economy the best chance to adapt to change. The world in which we live is beset by change: technological, environmental, and political; all of these have their economic implications. Change is never costless. In general, statist prescriptions involve postponing change by delaying its effects. Thus, in the 1970s, we resisted the rise in the price of oil by imposing price controls and complex allocation procedures. The result was gas lines and a delayed adjustment to the economic reality of higher prices. Intervention was inefficient in two ways: we had to waste resources in order to delay the effect of change and, in the end, we had an economy that was less fuel efficient than it otherwise would have been.

Because the prospect of change is often frightening to many people, there is always a demand for state intervention. Today, the term *regulation* is passé, because regulation has manifestly failed. The current interventionist phrase is *partnership*. No profit-making business ever voluntarily makes the government its partner. The government as partner will play the same role as the government as regulator. It will slow economic progress by forcing economic decision makers to adopt less efficient means of doing their jobs. Thus, any change to a more statist set of economic policies will soon produce the kind of economic decline we witnessed in the 1970s. Any political move to enhance the economic power of the state is therefore likely to be short-lived. As institutions, it is best for universities to ignore the possible vagaries of the four-year presidential cycle and plan for the long-term trend toward individualism, which will last well into the next century.

In my view, there are few institutions that will benefit as much from this long-term intellectual trend as the universities of America. After all, the training of the individual is our reason for being. Although some may argue that the trend to a more technical society will require more emphasis on the kind of expert training offered by technical schools, I disagree. In my view, the intellectual and practical triumph of individualistic economic policies is custom made for a liberal arts curriculum.

The purpose of the liberal arts is to train the individual how to think, how to approach a problem from a variety of points of view. A world in which society is exposed to the full force of economic change is one in which creativity and thought will be at a premium. Creativity will be an economic alternative to simply bearing the costs of change. I shall reserve until later my discussion of the specific changes universities must make to cope with this intellectual change, but the triumph of individualist economic policies is one aspect of the current economic revolution that we all should welcome without hesitation.

To a large extent, our political leaders recognize the role of education in training decision makers to make the most of individualistic economic policies. Both candidates for president in the 1988 election stressed the importance of education in their view of the future. They realized that our economy requires a workforce that is more than just literate and numerate. It is easy to realize that in the new economic and intellectual environment, the greatest economic progress will be attained by those societies that have educated their populations to be flexible, adaptable, and creative. Today, whole new technologies emerge in a matter of years, not decades. Workers who cannot adapt to the latest changes, to emerging technologies, will be a permanent drag on the economy. If the need for future economic growth were the sole criterion of public policy, the future of public support for education would be bright indeed. We could easily expect public funds to pour into our institutions. Unfortunately, this will not be the case. A second aspect of the reemergence of economic individualism will significantly alter the trend in government funding of higher education.

THE FISCAL REVOLUTION

The economic revolution in policymaking from statist to individualistic solutions is not limited to intellectual discussion. Statist prescriptions are not only facing intellectual bankruptcy; they are also constrained by the fact that government has reached its fiscal limits. In the next few years, federal tax revenue will account for roughly 20 percent of GNP, a new record. Indeed, in the next budget cycle, federal taxes will take an even larger share of national output than they did during the Second World War, when the nation was fully mobilized. Counting state and local revenue, roughly one-third of the nation's output is channeled through government; that proportion is higher than it has ever been.

For reasons I will discuss later, we will be unable to expand the scope of government to any significant extent.

There is some evidence that even the current level of government spending is unsustainable. To some degree, our current level of spending is not being financed by a permanent source of domestic revenue, but by borrowing from abroad. From both a national and an international perspective, most of this borrowing was sound. However, it cannot continue indefinitely. The international economic situation combines with domestic political and economic realities to make further expansion of the government's share of the economy untenable. Let us consider why this is so, beginning with the international economic situation.

First, in spite of all of the political rhetoric to the contrary, America has not lost its competitive edge in the world. Those who call for a more protectionist trade posture are not only risking an international trade war reminiscent of the 1930s; they are also calling for policies which are likely to hurt this country more than any other. In the last five years, American industry has undergone a major restructuring which has greatly reduced the overhead cost of production. In addition, the recent decline in the exchange rate of the dollar has made American industries especially competitive in the world market. If the world economy, particularly international trade, continues to grow at a rapid clip, the primary beneficiary will be the exporting industries in the world's newest low-cost producer—the U.S.A. A revival of protectionism would make the painful restructuring of American industry in the last five years largely an exercise in futility.

In response to those who think that American industry is being undermined from abroad, consider the following facts. In the last five years, the U.S. economy as a whole grew 22 percent, while industrial production grew 29 percent, and manufacturing output rose a startling 37 percent. In other words, our economy is becoming REindustrialized, not DEindustrialized, as some would have you believe. The share of national output from manufacturing and industry is increasing, not decreasing. This story is most impressive when placed in an international context. During the same five-year period, industrial production in Europe grew only 11.5 percent. Even the much vaunted Japanese have had only a 27 percent increase in industrial production. Let me repeat that fact for emphasis. In the last five years, American industrial growth has outpaced that of Japan.

The international trading situation has more to do with education than one would think. Although we rarely think of ourselves as such, American education is one of America's most successful export industries. Although precise figures are unavailable, foreign students probably account for between 10 and 15 percent of the students at America's institutions of higher education. Thus, the threat of protectionism is not only a threat to the world economy, but will also have a direct impact on higher education. A shrinkage of world trade means that both our imports and our exports will decline, including the number of foreign students attending American universities.

The underlying reason for our trade deficit has nothing to do with foreign barriers to our goods. If this were the case, the 20 percent growth in our exports to the rest of the world in the last year would not have been possible. Foreign trade barriers are largely a scapegoat used by those who seek to advance the cause of protectionism. The real reason for the international trade deficit was the other side of the international financial ledger: flows of capital into America.

During much of the 1980s, America was the world's most profitable place to invest. Falling inflation and attractive interest rates coupled with a political environment which was highly favorable to business produced an unprecedented demand for American assets by foreigners. The flip side of buying more goods and services than we sell is that we sell more U.S. assets to foreigners than we buy of their assets. American assets were selling at a premium while foreign goods and services were a bargain.

The press has called the process of foreign purchase of American assets making America a net "debtor" nation. That categorization is largely inaccurate. Much of the foreign investment in the United States has been of the equity sort—Toyota plants in Tennessee, for example. However, this type of investment leads to the xenophobic charge that foreigners are buying up America. The charge is, of course, exaggerated. But the more pertinent reply is, so what? As the world's greatest overseas investor for four decades, it is hypocritical, to say the least, for America to argue that people shouldn't invest in other countries' economies.

Besides, a more interdependent world is probably a good thing, not a bad thing. The old saying, that armies do not cross borders over which trade flows, has a good deal of empirical evidence to support it. The same can be said of the ownership of capital assets in other countries. It is almost inconceivable that a nation would attack its neighbor when its own assets might be destroyed in the fighting. This free movement of ideas, people, and capital is part of the worldwide reemergence of economic individualism. It allows assets to be invested where they are most productive while increasing the perception that we are all residents of the same planet. On balance, it is quite clear that foreign investment in America is, on net, a good thing.

An issue that is open to debate is whether we have used wisely the money received from selling our assets. A good deal of the foreign investment in America has involved the purchase of Treasury securities.

To some extent, we have sold assets, and issued debt, to finance the government budget deficit.

Going into debt, or selling off assets, is not always a bad thing to do, either for a household or for a country. To the extent that our budget deficit goes to accumulate productive and long-lived capital, borrowing is an appropriate method of finance. Purchases of roads, airports, and aircraft carriers should be amortized over many years, and not counted as spending in the year they are purchased. Borrowing to purchase assets which yield a return over many years is a sound practice. It is also appropriate for the government to engage in deficit spending at times of high unemployment. During the first half of the decade, macro-economic conditions were such that borrowing to finance government spending was appropriate from a macroeconomic perspective.

Foreign exchange markets have a means for signaling whether borrowing is appropriate or inappropriate. Until 1986, most of the debt bought by foreigners was purchased by the private sector; that is, by individuals who found lending to America profitable. International bankers, like their domestic counterparts, make loans only if they expect that the project they are lending for will be profitable enough to return both the principal and interest. In fact, the demand to lend to America and invest in American assets drove the dollar to record highs.

Since 1986, net foreign lending to America has occurred principally through government-run central banks. Unlike their private sector counterparts, a central bank's objective is not profit, but achieving certain macroeconomic objectives, notably to keep its country's currency undervalued. However, both the patience and the resources of foreign central banks is limited. German and Japanese central bankers, and by extension German and Japanese taxpayers, have literally lost tens of billions of dollars in the past two years buying American Treasury bills in an effort to prop up the value of the dollar.

Under current terms, America has probably reached its credit limit. We have three options. First, we can pay foreigners more for lending to us by raising U.S. interest rates. The risk is that higher interest rates would slow down domestic economic growth and might cause a recession. Second, we can let the dollar go lower. This makes American assets cheaper and thus continues the process of selling U.S. assets, only at a better price from the point of view of foreigners. Third, we can stop borrowing as much. From a policy perspective, this means reducing the federal budget deficit, which currently consumes between one-quarter and one-third of all the funds available to the U.S. economy, both foreign and domestic.

The Bush Administration has apparently chosen the last course. By establishing its willingness to endure the pains of sequestration under the Gramm-Rudman law, it was quite successful at forcing meaningful deficit reduction for the 1990 fiscal year. Furthermore, every indication is that it will propose a deficit of just $64 billion for the 1991 fiscal year.

Confidence on the part of foreigners that America will remain a profitable place to invest underlies our current prosperity. Threats of retaliatory trade legislation, re-regulation of American industry, or the adding of new taxes and costs to American business are sure ways to shake that confidence. Similarly, foreigners must be reassured that we will begin to tackle our fiscal policy problems. International economic constraints thus reinforce the limits on further government expansion caused by the reemergence of economic individualism.

The impending decline in our ability to borrow from abroad compels some action on the federal budget deficit. It is important to stress that although our current budget deficit problem is large, it is not insurmountable. The deficit does not exist for economic reasons, but for political ones. The country is stalled on a political consensus that favors high spending but doesn't want to pay for it. To a greater extent then ever before, one of our political parties sees itself as the taxpayers' party while the other sees itself as the party of those who need government assistance.

The solution will involve a slower rate of spending growth than we have taken for granted in the past. Because of the laws of budgetary arithmetic, it is inevitable that if we are to reduce our budget deficit, the vast bulk of policy changes will involve slower spending growth rather than the addition of new and higher taxes.

Consider why this is the case. Under current economic assumptions, the economy will grow about 7 percent per year, 4 points of which will be inflation and 3 will be real economic growth. Under current tax law, taxes will rise about 9 percent or about $72 billion per year. Spending is also scheduled to rise about $72 billion per year, leaving the deficit unchanged at about $150 billion.

If we simply restrain spending growth to the rate of inflation, 4 percent, spending will rise only by about $36 billion per year. The deficit will fall by about $36 billion per year and will be completely eliminated in four or five years. Thus, simply restraining the growth of spending to the rate of inflation gets rid of the deficit.

By contrast, the largest percent tax increase in postwar American history was a 10 percent income tax surcharge. Under current law, such an increase would raise about $50 billion per year by fiscal 1992, or about one-third of the deficit. Thus, even the equivalent of the largest tax increase in history will take care of only one-third of the deficit while restraining spending growth to the rate of inflation will permanently eliminate the deficit. Logic strongly suggests that if we are going to solve our deficit problem, it is spending restraint that will accomplish most of our success. Taxes will be at most a peripheral solution.

The logic of our international trading situation also suggests that spending restraint, not increased taxes, will be most beneficial. Recall that one of our problems is that we have to borrow from abroad. If the taxes that are levied to reduce the deficit come out of domestic savings rather than domestic consumption, the net borrowing situation of the country will remain unchanged. Thus, proposals to "soak the rich and the corporations" will do very little to solve our national borrowing problem. They are precisely the kinds of proposals which undermine foreign confidence. So, if we are to be economically successful, any taxes we impose must come out of some consumption-oriented activity, and so must fall primarily on the middle class. Thus, even the kind of modest deficit reduction that a tax increase might permit would be politically very difficult.

A tax increase will be difficult, but one which produces revenue by raising the tax rates enacted in the 1986 tax reform seems even more unlikely. Congress is probably not going to be willing to tinker with its historic compromise of base broadening and rate reduction. As Senator Bradley has argued, let the country experience the new 28 percent rate for a while.

If we are going to raise taxes, but not rates, then currently untaxed activities are going to have to be brought into the tax base. This has the political attraction of being called "closing loopholes" rather than increasing taxes. In addition, most of these alleged loopholes are for consumption-oriented activities and will not significantly affect national saving and investment. The Ways and Means Committee of the House of Representatives compiled a list of possible tax increases to help meet the revenue target in last year's Congressional Budget Resolution. The resulting 291-page document is the menu for any future tax increase. It also indicates why anyone concerned with the future of higher education should not favor a new tax bill given the current political makeup of the Congress.

Tucked away near the back is a proposal to tax the investment income of currently tax-exempt organizations. The wording of the argument in favor of this proposal is particularly interesting: "In times of large Federal budget deficits, all organizations that benefit from the expenditures of the Federal Government should be called upon to contribute to reducing the budget deficits."

For those who think that these educational institutions should be exempt because they did not receive any federal funds, the view in the document of what constitutes a government benefit is made broad enough to include them. According to the document, among the benefits for which these institutions should be taxed are national defense, the regulation of the banking system, and the maintenance of the interstate transportation network. There is no escape. Congress could get about $6 billion per year from this idea.

In my view, an even more devastating proposal is the plan to limit the value of all itemized deductions, including the deduction for charitable contributions. Under this plan, itemized deductions could be taken against the 15 percent bracket only. Congress could take in about $24 billion by this action.

The 1986 tax bill sharply reduced the incentives for charitable giving. In 1981, the federal tax expenditure for charitable giving amounted to $11 billion. In 1988, it was at about $9 billion. In the interim, the economy has grown about 80 percent, cutting the tax expenditure from 0.45 percent of personal income to only 0.23 percent of personal income. The decision in the 1986 bill to treat the appreciated portion of gifts of assets as a tax preference was precedent shattering. Unfortunately, these actions are an indication of congressional attitudes, and indicate that higher education will be adversely affected by any future tax bill.

In addition to the potential taxation of endowment income and a reduction in the tax incentives for charitable giving, a further likely tax change is the taxation of unrelated business income. This is the infamous UBIT, or unrelated business income tax. Under a reasonable interpretation of the UBIT principle, any activity engaged in by a nonprofit entity that is not directly tied to its nonprofit mission could be subject to tax.

It is true that the nonprofit sector is not wholly on the side of the angels on the issue of UBIT. The YMCA is a frequently cited example. In the past, the "Y" was engaged in the charitable activity of promoting physical fitness and good health among urban workers. Today, physical fitness is in fashion, and health centers are a booming and highly profitable business. Today's YMCA is usually as posh as its for-profit competitors. No one has done anything nefarious. Society has changed. An activity that once could be funded only as a charitable endeavor is now in such demand that it can be provided in the profit-driven marketplace. The tax law's definition of what constitutes legitimate tax-exempt activity is bound to change with the times.

Given the inevitability of change and current congressional attitudes, I think it is time that we consider a thoroughly heretical idea. With the exception of charitable donations, which must be handled separately, I think we should consider having our colleges and universities, and all of their functions, treated as taxable corporations.

Before you start melting tar and plucking feathers, let's consider what the profit-and-loss statement of a taxable higher education organization would look like. On the one hand, our charitable activity, education, is a big money loser, and no one proposes taxing that. On the other hand, our institutions run numerous activities, including renting housing, holding portfolios in our endowments, and the like, that are unrelated, and generally profitable. With all activities combined, it is a rare institution indeed that makes money. The profits on UBIT activities and income from endowments are usually more than offset by losses in the educational part of the enterprise. This would be especially true as universities are forced to adopt business depreciation schedules for their classroom buildings and related structures. So, as taxable corporations, our institutions would rarely, if ever, pay taxes.

However, the current congressional moves to tax our endowments and unrelated business activities are targeted at the profitable half of the business with no allowance for the fact that these profits are used to cover the losses incurred in educating our nation's children. Taken as a whole, our institutions owe no tax. But, left to its own devices, a revenue hungry Congress will divide and conquer, taxing only our profitable activities, while leaving untouched the money-losing education side of our business. Faced with this possibility, heresy may start to catch on.

I can only conclude that any likely tax legislation will be bad for education. Furthermore, the relentless budget arithmetic I mentioned earlier makes rescue on the appropriations side extremely unlikely. The best we can hope for is that federal outlays for education will keep pace with inflation. Remember, to balance the budget in four to five years, federal outlays as a whole can rise only as fast as inflation.

Money for education is unlikely to come from defense cuts. Even savage cuts to our long-term defense capability will provide only marginal assistance to social spending. We are now entering our fourth budgetary year of constant real defense expenditures. In my view, the combined demands of national security and budgetary restraint will keep the defense budget in the mode of constant or declining real expenditures. However, large declines in defense spending should not be expected for the next few years. There is simply not enough money available in further defense spending cuts to allow for more spending on education programs.

Competition for funds on the domestic side of the budget is intense. While Social Security pension payments rise only about as fast as inflation, Medicare payments grow seemingly without limit. Even under the Reagan Administration, the real increase in Medicare spending was nearly twice the real increase in defense spending. When one considers the tough choices that any president faces on the budget, it's a wonder that anyone runs for the office. Expectations that political change will produce a windfall of education spending are sure to be disappointed.

The fiscal aspects of the current revolution in economic policy making will require a change in the strategy that higher education has relied on for the past 40 years. Since the GIs returned from the Second World War, higher education has looked increasingly to the federal government as a source for funding. The government provided us with both a favorable tax climate and regular increases in real support for education. In spite of all the rhetoric about the value of education, the President and the Congress simply are not in a position to continue the policies of the past, much less expand on them. While some well-designed, low-cost programs, such as educational savings bonds, are likely to be enacted, the overall level of real federal spending will not increase for the forseeable future.

The effects of this change need not all be bad. Federal funding is becoming associated with an increasingly burdensome set of rules, the potential impact of which is only now becoming clear. Consider, for example, the recent congressional reversal of the Supreme Court in the Grove City case, known as the Civil Rights Restoration Act. The Court had held that non-compliance with federal regulations by a part of an institution would jeopardize federal support for only that part of the institution. Grove City College had provided unequal athletic facilities for its male and female students. Thus, the Court held that the cutoff in funds would be limited to that money used by the school's sports department. The Congress reversed that decision, providing that all support, including federal research support, student loan programs, and direct federal aid, was jeopardized if any part of the institution failed to comply.

One can only wonder what will happen to support of universities when we have an administration which is more expansive and aggressive in its definition of what constitutes a civil rights violation. Is equal funding of male and female teams in each sport to be required—football, for example? To pick an example that has made the popular press, what is the University of California system to do with its racial quota system that necessitates unequal standards for white, black, and oriental students? What will all of our institutions do about the difficult problem of recruiting minority faculty members? Or, consider a problem that has only been made clear to me this year: equal education for handicapped students. It's the law of the land. For the first time in all my years of teaching, I have a blind student. The difficulty in conveying graphical concepts to her, which form the basis of the course material, is really testing my pedagogical limits. In spite of my best efforts, and the efforts of my staff, I think that a good case can be made that she is not receiving an equal education, even though she is commanding a disproportionately large amount of resources.

The current expanse of state power means that every university in the country and their students can lose all their federal support if any one of the many protected groups in the law can establish unequal treatment in some facet of the university's services. In my view, relying on the notion of the reasonableness of enforcement is foolish when the law itself mandates totally unreasonable penalties. The reemergence of economic individualism will gradually cause an end to the practice of defining individuals by their characteristics rather than as individuals. In the meantime, the risks to our institutions in the currently excessive use of state power to enforce collectivist rights will be enormous. The less we are dependent upon the goodwill of the state and its largesse, the better off we will be.

ECONOMIC INDIVIDUALISM AND THE PRODUCT WE OFFER

If our institutions are going to receive less funding from Uncle Sam, where will we look for support? The answer is obvious: our customers. Other nonprofit agencies such as the YMCA have already adapted to the changing environment by catering to society's new tastes. Our institutions, like the YMCA, are in the midst of a social revolution that we have generally failed to recognize. Education is going to become increasingly similar to a for-profit business in the years ahead. The institutions that will survive and prosper are those that can provide the market what it needs. This means making the customer happy.

As an indication of this trend, note that currently a majority of federal education loans are given to students attending proprietary schools, not the traditional nonprofit university. These proprietary schools are filling market niches which our more traditional institutions have failed to cover. The students going to these schools are there for one reason: they think the product offered will more than pay for itself in terms of career advancement and higher pay.

The impending decline in the relative importance of federal assistance as a source of revenue means we are going to have to care more about what our customers, the students, think of the product being offered. As more of the burden is shifted on to them, they will become increasingly critical of whether they are getting their money's worth. Only institutions that offer a product that pays for itself, from the student's point of view, are going to prosper in the years ahead.

Some see this as a threat to the traditional liberal arts curriculum. I disagree. Many of the most plaintive arguments against current trends in our schools, such as Alan Bloom's *The Closing of the American Mind*, propose remedies which stress the liberal arts even more. For example,

Bloom proposes a two-year study of the Great Books. We educators have always asserted that the liberal arts teach students how to think, how to attack complex problems from multiple points of view. As our economy puts an increasing premium on creativity and innovation, a curriculum which teaches what the liberal arts are supposed to teach will become increasingly valuable.

While the liberal arts are not threatened, some liberal arts courses, which are long on talk and short on thought, will become increasingly irrelevant. Students are going to demand their money's worth as it is increasingly their money that is paying for their education. Our customers are growing restless, and will become more so as time goes on. Traditionally, universities have been the centers of protest about conditions outside our walls. In general, we have adapted by taking a tolerant attitude. But, while it is easy to tolerate protest in the abstract, it is quite difficult to take when it hits close to home. Already there have been some student protests about this issue and some of America's future investigative reporters have attacked the quality of teaching of some professors. Expect the trend to grow. Most important, do not confuse the issue of teaching competence with ideological issues. Universities must defend academic freedom and must be pillars of racial, religious, and ideological tolerance. That does not mean that they have to defend incompetence. Those universities that listen to student concerns about teaching and that do not try to hide behind other excuses will be the ones to prosper.

The fear of consumer protest is not the only economic motivation for institutions of higher education to start changing their practices. The emergence of the home computer and the VCR pose a technological challenge to the way teaching is done in America. If education is viewed as simply the absorption of material, then the days of our colleges and universities are numbered. One can easily develop and market instructional material on video cassettes and interactive computer programs for less than the $18,000 our schools are currently charging. The information age we are now living in is one in which the dissemination of information is cheap. High-cost producers of information will not survive.

The sharp reduction in the cost of disseminating information is one of the key reasons for the reemergence of economic individualism. Today it is possible for ordinary workers to obtain easily the quantity and quality of information that previously required a sophisticated and expensive bureaucracy to gather. Throughout the world, individuals will be capable of making the decisions that used to be relegated to centers of power. This economic revolution is what is going to cause the demand for education to increase. These newly empowered individuals are going to demand the kind of background that permits them to make the maximum creative use of the information at their disposal. As a whole, the importance of the role that education plays in society will reach a new high.

We cannot be passive. We cannot expect the rising demand for our services to be an endorsement of the current way we deliver our product. Economics is going to force us to define our role differently. We can no longer be mere disseminators of knowledge. The reason to go to a college rather than watch VCR tapes is not a difference in content. It is a difference in motivation. A live human being in front of a classroom can motivate learning in a way that someone on a tape cannot. Those schools that hire faculty based on the capacity to motivate the learners will successfully compete against VCR tapes. Nobody is going to pay $18,000 per year to listen to a lecturer who is as dry as a computer program. Considering the current personnel policies of universities, this economic challenge is going to be the toughest one for them to meet.

The 1990s hold out great promise for both our economy and for higher education. The rapid pace of technological advance will place a premium on workers who can adapt to, and help advance, the new technologies. This can only be good news for educational institutions that train workers to be creative. At the same time, the federal government will be preoccupied with its own budgetary concerns, and unable to assist us in adapting to these new opportunities. Governmental preoccupation with itself may actually produce still faster economic growth as the dead hand of the regulator will be less likely to inhibit economic change. However, we must not be misled into thinking that the new technologies will affect only the world outside the university walls. As the centers of the information age, we are going to be challenged more than most. Those institutions which listen to, and adapt to, the message of the market will prosper. Those that do not will not survive the twenty-first century.

This paper is dedicated to the memory of F. Gordon Lindsey, lifelong educator, a former teacher and administrator at Clarkson College, who died while this text was nearing completion. He would have found many of the thoughts expressed here to resemble his own, these words having been inspired by his views on the proper role of an educator in our changing society.

2

THE U.S. ECONOMY AND HIGHER EDUCATION

RICHARD S. ECKAUS

My task is to provide a vision of the future economic environment as it will affect higher education in the United States. To a considerable extent, however, all that I will be able to do is to describe the constraints within which future economic developments will occur and how those will condition the outcomes. Working out the specific consequences for higher education would require research that was not part of my charge. So, without apologies, I take up my assigned task, but with the warning, in the words of an old Chinese proverb: "Reading the stars is hard; catching them is even harder."

Economists are often asked to make predictions, as if we possessed crystal balls. We don't; nonetheless we respond. We respond because all of us, economists or not, must look into the future as we make our plans as individuals and as members of our communities. Making plans for the future is necessary because, for a number of reasons, societies and economies are not perfectly adaptable from year to year.

Educational systems, perhaps particularly systems of higher education, have a good deal of inertia. Faculties are difficult both to expand and to contract; most facilities cannot be built quickly or adapted easily. Thus, the projections of the future that would be most useful for education policy are longer term projections, so that there would be time to adapt to them. Such projections would extend over the next three to fifteen years perhaps. Yet long-term projections are much more difficult to make than projections for the next six to twelve months.

The first step is to describe, briefly but reasonably comprehensively, just where the U.S. economy stands today. That provides the basis for indicating the boundaries within which it will move over the next ten years or so. More specific implications for higher education can then be taken up. An effective way of organizing our approach to this last task is in a demand and supply framework. This structure has the advantages of being both intuitive and, as necessary and with suitable elaborations, rigorous. A possible source of difficulty is that one institution's or agent's supply conditions can influence another institution's demand. For example, in higher education, decisions by public institutions to expand or contract their offerings will affect the demands on private institutions. We will try to draw attention to these interactions where necessary.

CURRENT CHARACTERISTICS OF THE U.S. ECONOMY
RECENT OVERALL PATTERNS

I will not try to provide an economic atlas of the U.S. economy, but a few facts will offer a setting for the main discussion.

For purposes of comparison, the pattern of overall growth rates in the United States since 1970 is presented in Chart 2.1, along with the growth rates of several other major industrialized countries. Most of the

CHART 2.1. COMPARATIVE GROWTH RATES (PERCENT)

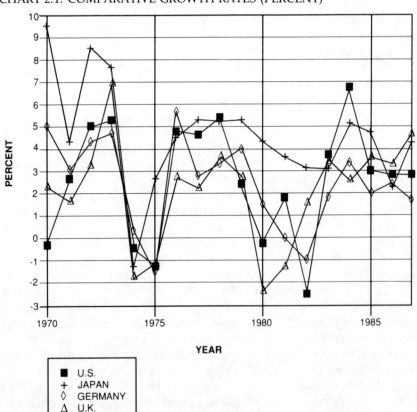

recent ups and downs reflect the two "oil price shocks" of the 1970s and the reactions to them. The United States was about at the middle of the pack in the 1970s.[1] But then the U.S. economy began to outperform the other economies in 1983 and 1984. Although the growth rates have declined since then, the recent overall record remains strong.

The comparative strength is particularly evident in Chart 2.2, which presents the rates of growth of employment.[2] In the two periods of expansion—in the 1970s and again in the 1980s—the U.S. economy has been strikingly more successful than the other economies in creating new jobs. Our understanding of this success is, at best, incomplete but

CHART 2.2. EMPLOYMENT GROWTH RATES (PERCENT)

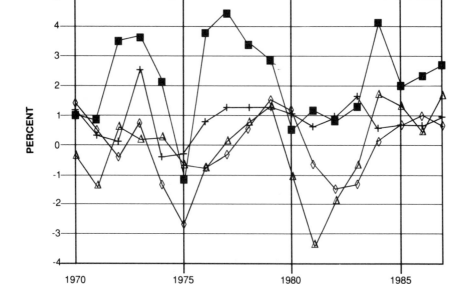

YEAR

■	U.S.
+	JAPAN
◊	GERMANY
Δ	U.K.

1. The source of the data in Chart 2.1 is *OECD Economic Outlook* 43 (June 1988), OECD, Paris.
2. The source of the data on the U.S. economy is, for the most part, *Economic Report of the President, 1988* (Washington, D.C.; U.S.Government Printing Office, January 1988).

the most widespread view is that it reflects the relative flexibility of U.S. wage and employment practices.

Chart 2.3 presents another aspect of employment growth: unemployment rates. Since there are differences in the definitions and reporting of unemployment among countries, the absolute levels are less informative, at least for present purposes, than are the trends. It is most striking that the U.S. unemployment rate began falling in 1982 and has continued downward since then. By comparison, unemployment rates have been rising in the other countries, except for a recent downward tick in England.

These charts paint a fairly glowing picture of the U.S. economy. Relatively few economists doubt that the performance has been due mostly to the very large federal deficits of the last seven years. It was not "supply-side" economics that did it. It was old-fashioned Keynesian deficit spending set off by a tax bill that reduced the share of taxes taken

CHART 2.3. UNEMPLOYMENT RATES (PERCENT)

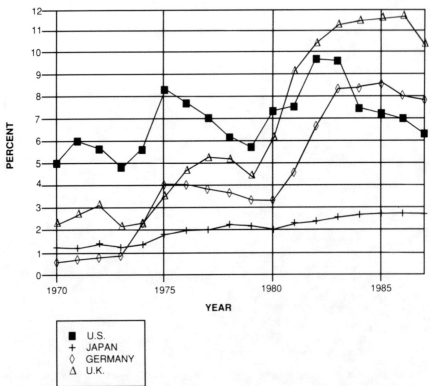

by the government plus a large increase in the share of output purchased by the government, mainly for military purposes.

The real growth was achieved by absorbing unemployed workers,
by increased utilization of capacity, and, after a slowdown in the mid-
1980s, by increased investment. Because of the low national savings
rate—aggravated by the federal deficit—a large part of the investment
was financed by foreign savings, which was the counterpart of the large
international current account deficit.

The deficit of the federal government and the trade deficit are both
shown in Chart 2.4. The federal deficits were, by current standards,
quite modest until the second half of the 1970s, when they increased
substantially. The rates of growth of the deficits accelerated in the early
1980s and have scarcely moved away from the unprecedented levels
reached in the mid-1980s.

CHART 2.4. FEDERAL AND INTERNATIONAL DEFICITS (BILLIONS OF
           DOLLARS)

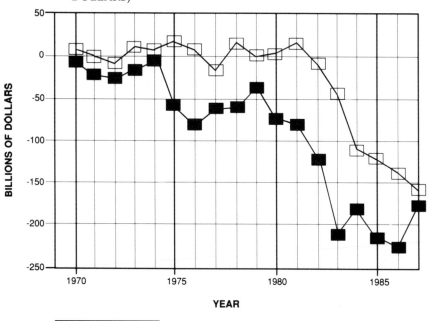

By comparison the international current account deficit did not start to deteriorate badly until 1983. Since that time, however, it has continued to grow, with a slackening of that growth in 1987. Recent statistics suggest that there will be a decline in the deficit in 1988, although it will remain high.

It was the particular combination of monetary and fiscal policies of the last seven years that generated the government budget and trade deficits. Relatively tight monetary policies were imposed by the Federal Reserve to create relatively high interest rates in order to prevent the federal deficits created by the 1981 tax reduction act from generating even more rapid economic expansion and inflationary pressures. The high interest rates, in turn, helped maintain the exchange rate of the U.S. dollar against foreign currencies. This, and the comparatively strong expansion of the U.S. economy as compared to the economies of many of the other industrialized countries, caused the trade deficits.

As inflationary pressures were reduced, the Federal Reserve was able to relax its monetary tightness and to lower interest rates. Without high interest rates, the attractiveness of the U.S. dollar declined and, in early 1986, the dollar started depreciating rapidly against other major currencies.

The consequence has been further expansion, led now not only by the federal deficits but also by export growth which has, in turn, stimulated more investment. This recent growth has been consistent with a falling trade deficit. It suggests the kind of growth that is possible in the future, even without the stimulus of large federal deficits.

Looking underneath the aggregate numbers, one may begin to have doubts about the economic success story. Chart 2.5 presents the median income of families and individuals in the labor force from 1970 to 1986. It is striking that, in spite of overall economic growth, it was only in 1986 that the median income of families climbed back to levels previously achieved in the 1970s. It is even more striking that the median income of individuals in 1986 was substantially lower than in 1973. There are several reasons for the differences between the patterns for families and individuals, one which is the increasing participation of women in the labor force but at relatively low income levels. This phenomenon also helps to explain the observation that, while per capita income has been rising, the median income of individuals in the labor force has been falling: an increasing proportion of the population is working and earning income, helping to raise the average income of the entire population.

What about some of the other warnings that we hear: that the United States is losing its technological leadership in critical areas of high technology and that we are backward in terms of both managerial and labor skills? There are no graphs or statistics that can readily throw light on these somewhat amorphous questions that nonetheless reflect critical issues. There are essays and studies, some of which, though best sellers, are only impressionistic. There are also serious scholars and studies that do give insightful information about particular sectors. However, hardly any of the studies are conclusive on the broadest levels at which the questions are posed. So we remain in the dark about potentially significant facts.

There are several different types of problems in evaluating the various gloomy assessments of the current state of the U.S. economy. First, because substantial groups of people have vested interests in the current situation, it is a useful public relations ploy to present any threat to their welfare as a threat to the general prosperity. Second, it is often difficult to distinguish the changes that signal long-term decline from the adaptations that are always necessary in an economy that is continually re-

CHART 2.5. MEDIAN INCOMES, FAMILIES AND INDIVIDUALS
(THOUSANDS, 1986 DOLLARS)

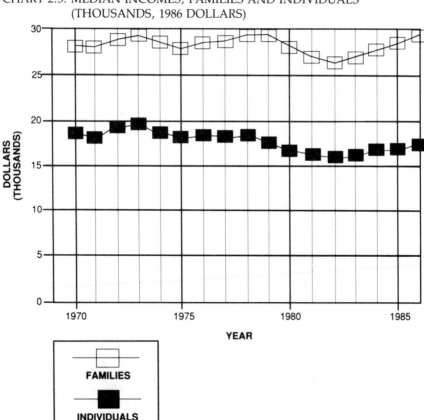

newing itself. This difficulty is partly because the new industries and new technologies that will replace the ones that decline or move away are almost never easily identifiable far in advance of their success.

An example often cited in the debate is the loss to Japan of our leading position in the production of random access memory chips. That shift has led to dark forecasts for the U.S. computer industry and all industries closely associated with it. The response of many economists is that

> this is simply the expected type of adjustment to real changes in international comparative advantage and to movements in the exchange rate of the U.S. dollar against foreign currencies;
>
> consumers will be better off because of the lower prices of imports;
>
> new industries will develop to replace the old; depreciation of the U.S. dollar will regain competitiveness for U.S. industry.

On the other hand, there are economists, as well as many businessmen and engineers, who believe that the problems have their source in "structural" features of the U.S. economy, that is, its fundamental characteristics. Some of those commonly cited are the following:

> the relatively low savings rate is, itself, partly responsible for high financial costs in the United States, in spite of the reputed efficiency of international financial markets;
>
> various provisions of the U.S. corporate income tax law also raise U.S. financial costs;
>
> the short planning horizon of U.S. managers makes them seek short-term advantages at the expense of their long-term industrial position.

SECTORAL PERFORMANCE

A change in the U.S. economy that has drawn a great deal of attention is the apparent long-term sectoral shift away from goods production toward the service sectors. In the 30 years from 1955 to 1985 the share of the gross national product originating in the goods producing sectors fell from 46 percent to 41 percent. In the same period, the share of the service sectors rose from 40 percent to 44 percent. However, there has recently been a change that may undo the apparent trend. In the three years since 1985, the share of goods production in the GNP has risen to 44 percent, although the share of the service sector has continued to increase to 46 percent.

The change in employment patterns had been more drastic than the change in output shares. In the early 1960s, about 30 percent of the labor force was employed in manufacturing and only 14 percent in the service sectors. Now, only about 19 percent of employment is in manufacturing and almost 24 percent is in services.

Output in the manufacturing sector has increased somewhat less than 2.5 times from 1960 to 1988, while manufacturing employment has increased by only one-eighth. By contrast, service output has increased slightly more than 2.5 times during the same period but employment in the service sectors has increased 3.4 times.

At least in retrospect, it should not have been surprising that this type of change would take place. Various studies have shown a higher responsiveness to increases in income of demands for the services of the educational and health sectors, for example, than demands for goods.

There has been speculation on the implications of this change for the nature of U.S. society, the character of U.S. cities, the structure of the labor force, even the returns to higher education. In some cases the changes have been dramatic. The personal and physical dislocations due to the decline of "smokestack" industries as well as some nondurable goods industries in the face of foreign competition are real and have been highlighted in any number of studies and articles.

The attention may be somewhat misleading, however. While the relative importance of manufacturing employment has fallen, the total number of workers in the sector has changed very little. Reductions in some sectors have been offset by expansion in other sectors, that is, the dislocations, though difficult and painful, are concentrated in particular sectors rather than requiring wholesale movements of labor from one sector to another. Nonetheless, because there is often a concentration of regional employment in a particular sector, the changes have often had a strong and focused local impact.

THE LONG-TERM OUTLOOK FOR THE ECONOMY

While economists are purported to be rather dour individuals, they are, like everyone else, really creatures of infatuations and enthusiasms. That, and an understandable desire for public attention, which can then be capitalized, produces long-term projections that frequently turn out to be quite wrong. It may help create the proper mood of skepticism about long-term forecasts to recall some popular apprehensions that have faded away. In the mid-1970s, there was the anxiety, promoted by the Club of Rome with the help of a number of economists, that the globe was about to run out of natural resources. The rapid increase in oil prices at the time helped make that diagnosis appear plausible. While there is still some cause for worry, it is not so extreme as first presented and the fears have now almost been forgotten.

Earlier, there was great concern in the 1960s about the loss of our accumulated stock of gold held in Fort Knox and the basement of the New York Federal Reserve Bank. Our ownership of gold was running down as the result of the continuing balance of payments deficits. While trade deficits are a continuing concern, today the anxiety about the loss of our gold stock seems an almost prehistoric fear.

There are similar scares now: the United States is in general decline; the Japanese are buying up the country; the manufacturing industries can no longer compete with the rest of the world and we are becoming a nation of hamburger flippers, etc. Like the other scares, there is just enough truth in the alarms to make them plausible. But many of these concerns, like the previous worries, are grossly overdone and/or susceptible to reasonable policies, if we are only willing to apply them.

There are, however, certain economic problems of the U.S. economy that are not overstated, that are real and deep. They may also be susceptible to economic policies, but there is profound disagreement on the content of those policies, reflecting not only professional ignorance among economists but significant political differences as well.

THE PROSPECTS FOR ECONOMIC GROWTH

We have an unusually long period of expansion behind us. There are some good reasons to expect that there may be a slowdown after such a long period of growth, including the fact that the federal government, under both Republicans and Democrats, has not been very fast on its feet in dealing with economic change. Yet there is no reason to believe that the U.S. economy is not capable of sustaining substantial growth rates and low unemployment rates in the future as in the recent past, although the basis for the growth must change.

For there to be growth over an extended period of time there must be some combination of use of more productive resources and increased productivity from the resources. Productive resources are conventionally classified by economists as natural resources, capital, and labor. Natural resources are part of the endowment; we can be more or less wise and efficient in their use, but cannot change what there are. Capital accumulation, through investment, requires saving, an issue that is dealt with in some detail below. "Labor" is not just raw strength and talent but refined skills and capabilities, to which education is a major contributor.

The saving necessary for investment must come from either domestic or foreign sources. On the domestic side, total saving is the sum of private household, business, and government saving. While state and local governments, in the aggregate, usually run surpluses, the federal government typically, is in deficit, that is, it is dissaving. Chart 2.6

shows *gross* savings rates as a proportion of GNP for the United States and some of the other major industrialized countries.[3] While there has been a general decline in savings rates over the last 20 years or so, the decline has been greatest in the United States.

Table 2.1 presents the *net* savings rates for the United States, distinguishing the sources of saving. The net savings rates are the gross rates minus the requirements for maintaining depreciated capital. Net private domestic saving has been declining, mainly because of the decline in household savings rates. State and local governments, in the aggregate, run small surpluses, but, as is well known, there has been a large increase in federal deficits in the 1980s. The increased recourse to foreign savings or net capital inflows has, therefore, been a result of the com-

CHART 2.6. COMPARATIVE SAVINGS RATES (PERCENT)

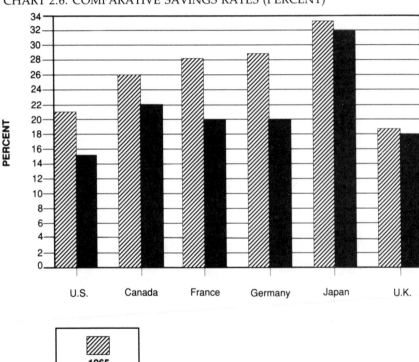

3. *World Development Report* (Washington, D.C.: World Bank, 1988), p. 231.

TABLE 2.1. U.S. NET SAVINGS AND INVESTMENT FLOWS AS PERCENTAGE OF GNP*

	NET PRIVATE DOMESTIC SAVING	STATE AND LOCAL GOVERNMENT SAVING	FEDERAL GOVERNMENT SAVING	TOTAL DOMESTIC SAVING	NET PRIVATE DOMESTIC INVESTMENT	NET FOREIGN SAVING
1950–59	7.5	−0.2	0.1	7.8	7.5	−0.3
1960–69	8.1	0.0	−0.3	7.8	7.1	−0.7
1970–79	8.1	0.9	−1.7	7.2	6.9	−0.3
1980	6.4	1.0	−2.2	5.2	4.9	−0.3
1981	6.6	1.1	−2.1	5.6	4.5	−0.3
1982	5.5	1.1	−4.6	2.0	2.0	−0.1
1983	5.7	1.4	−5.2	1.9	3.1	0.0
1984	6.8	1.7	−4.5	4.0	6.6	1.2
1985	5.7	1.6	−4.9	2.4	5.1	2.6
1986	5.3	1.3	−4.8	1.8	5.1	2.7
1987	4.3	1.0	−3.4	1.9	5.3	3.3
						3.4

*Congressional (Budget Office, The Economic and Budget Outlook 1989–1993, 1988 Annual Report (Washington, D.C.: U.S. Government Printing Office, 1988), p. 5.

bined effects of the decline in private saving and growth in federal deficits. In effect, foreign saving to help support U.S. investment has been provided to the United States when foreigners accepted our IOUs for a substantial portion of our imports.

There are at least four different positions among economists with respect to the dangers to our future growth and prosperity created by the low U.S. savings rates. The gloomiest assessment is, roughly, as follows:

> There is a lot to worry about. The low national savings rate, resulting mainly from the large federal deficits, is a major obstacle to U.S. growth. The country needs to invest on a much larger scale in order to increase national productivity and, consequentially, individual incomes. Conceivably we could continue to use foreign savings for investment, add to our foreign debt, and induce foreigners to support this by further depreciation of the U.S. dollar. Eventually this would lead us into grave exchange rate and capital flow problems, and "eventually" might not take more than a few years.

There is no doubt that investment is necessary at a higher rate in order to increase and improve the capital used by U.S. labor and enhance U.S. competitiveness in world trade. The data given above on the decline in average nonagricultural earnings essentially reflects the low rate of growth of labor productivity. The alternative of relying on foreign saving means, essentially, trying to sell an increasing proportion of the U.S. economy to foreigners. It is not national chauvinism that argues against this but rather a view that we do not want to accept the increasingly unfavorable terms of trade that would be implied if foreigners continued to finance our investment at the rates necessary.

Another side to the argument is more or less as follows:

> Don't worry. As long as the foreign saving is used for domestic investment rather than consumption and the return on the investment is greater than the interest rate paid on the debt, we can always get what we need from foreign sources. There is no permanent harm to the U.S. economy from having foreigners hold an increasing share of our assets.

The logic of the argument is sound. It is the assumptions that are questioned. It is difficult to guarantee that foreign savings will finance investment rather than consumption. If it is investment that is financed, and the return is higher than the interest rate, and, if there is no special scarcity of foreign exchange that interferes with the repatriation of profits abroad, then the argument follows.

However, there do seem to be limits to the willingness of foreigners to provide their savings to us. The depreciation of the U.S. dollar starting in 1987 was taken by many observers as a clear signal that the rest of the world was not going to continue to accept our IOUs and provide their savings to the United States on the same terms as in the past. The danger in this approach is that we copy the worst aspects of the common Latin American model as typified by Argentina, Brazil, and Mexico. We would not generate the same type of debt crisis that they generated, if our foreign debt was not primarily foreign bank loans. But the effect on our exchange rates would be the same. If foreigners forced repayment of their loans, the U.S. dollar would have to depreciate far enough to persuade the foreigners to use their dollars to buy U.S. assets.

A third alternative position in the debate is this:

> Don't worry. As long as the U.S. economy continues to expand reasonably quickly, we will grow out of the government deficits as tax revenues will increase more rapidly than expenditures. Growth will also stimulate private savings.

This, too, has logic and some facts on its side. Growth is not quite a universal panacea for economic ailments, but it certainly reduces their burden. It is true that accelerated economic growth will reduce the federal deficit and that, itself, would increase the overall savings rate. It is less obvious that it would increase the personal savings rate. There is also a real question as to whether economic growth can be maintained, although there is, perhaps, no more question about this than about the feasibility and success of policies to increase private savings rates.

The final alternative is this:

> Hunker down! We can get along with low growth based on the relatively low U.S. savings rate, with an international trade balance achieved with the right choice of the dollar's exchange rate and, therefore, without recourse to foreign savings. The important thing is not to get into international trade and payments problems that are not viable and would require traumatic adjustments to overcome.

That is not an attractive alternative for several reasons. Low growth rates provide fewer personal opportunities for individual advancement as well as smaller average increments in available goods and services. While the U.S. society is unusually open, there are still important groups of people whose opportunities have been quite restricted and many persons who still live in poverty. Redressing these inequities will be easier in a growing, rather than a stagnant economy.

The operative consequences of the first three positions, at least, need not be so different, although their relative emphases would be. In the latter two positions, there would not be so much worry about new measures to stimulate private savings in the United States and, presumably, there would be less willingness to sacrifice public undertakings to reduce the government deficit.

Since the "federal deficit problem" looms so large as an overall constraint and has particular significance for public education programs as well, it is worth some additional attention here. The federal deficits have a number of sources, but one of the most important is the tax reduction act of 1981, which lowered federal tax revenues below the level they would otherwise have achieved. The second important element is the steadily increasing importance of federal entitlement programs.

Federal tax revenues have actually increased since 1981, in part due to successive tax bills that have raised revenues after the big reduction in the tax bill of 1981. Federal tax revenues as a share of GNP are now at the levels of the late 1970s and, roughly, only about one-half of one percent below the ratios prevailing before the 1981 tax act.

Federal expenditures have increased more rapidly, as indicated by the growth in the federal deficit. A large part of that increase has been due to the rapid growth in military expenditures, but a large part is also due to the growth in entitlement and other mandatory spending programs. It is the latter set of expenditures that makes the deficit seem so intractable.

While it is clear what military expenditures are, the meaning of entitlement and mandatory spending programs is not so obvious. These are programs that

> pay benefits to any person, business, or unit of government that seeks payments and meets the eligibility rules set by the law. The Congress thus controls spending for these programs indirectly, by choosing the eligibility criteria and the benefit formula, rather than directly through the appropriation process.[4]

Examples are Medicaid, food stamps, supplemental security income, family support, veterans' pensions, and child nutrition.

Chart 2.7 indicates the changes that have occurred in the relative shares of the government budget devoted to the major categories of expenditure. The major expansion in entitlement programs came in the early 1970s. Their share of the total budget has hardly increased since the mid-1970s. The share of the budget going to national defense expenditures decreased during the 1970s, but rose substantially in the 1980s. The proportion of the budget absorbed by the payment of interest has risen sharply in the 1980s due to the sizable increases in federal deficits. Nondefense, discretionary expenditures—including educational expenditures—have been squeezed hard in the 1980s.

To indicate the intractable nature of the budget problem, the usual procedure is to calculate the tax revenues associated with alternative economic growth scenarios. These are then compared with projections of government expenditures, including those projections of discretion-

---

4. Congressional Budget Office, *The Economic and Budget Outlook: Fiscal Years 1989–1993, 1988 Annual Report* (Washington, D.C.: U.S. Government Printing Office, 1988).

ary expenditures that require annual appropriations, expenditures on entitlement programs, and interest payments on the government debt. The results are always substantial deficits, even if the projections of discretionary expenditures are quite moderate. The usual lesson is that there is no avoiding the persistence of substantial deficits and these, in turn, will make it impossible to expand discretionary programs, such as educational assistance.

Table 2.2 presents a set of projections by the Congressional Budget Office, an agency set up to provide information to the Congress and widely respected as a nonpartisan group.

The alternative projections will make one more or less depressed with respect to the potential freedom of action of the government to expand its educational assistance, depending on one's own economic forecasts and political preferences. It is clear that lower growth is bad and higher growth would be better. Inflation would also improve the

CHART 2.7. FEDERAL OUTLAYS BY MAJOR CATEGORY (SHARE OF TOTAL)

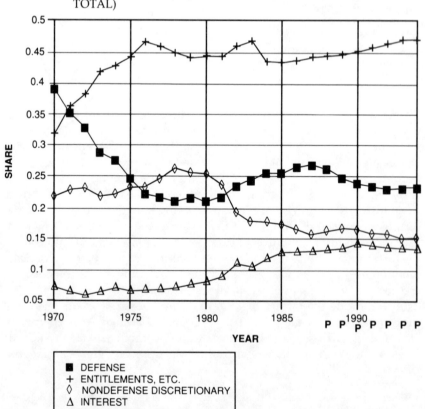

DEFENSE
+ ENTITLEMENTS, ETC.
◊ NONDEFENSE DISCRETIONARY
Δ INTEREST
P PROJECTIONS

deficit picture because not all tax and spending provisions are indexed to the rate of inflation.

The slightest familiarity with the current political scene suggests that it will be difficult to persuade the U.S. citizenry to pay more taxes. If taxes are not increased, however, the consequence will be continuing deficits and tight expenditure programs, at least until sufficient growth and/or inflation reduces deficit levels. Moreover, if there are lessons to be learned from other countries about entitlement programs, it is that they are inexorably persistent. However, judgments of this type are essentially political and, as an economist, the author can claim no special expertise in forecasting how much in taxes the U.S. citizenry will agree to pay for government services. As one among many citizens, I will only report that political events have a way of surprising even the professionals.

TABLE 2.2. BASELINE BUDGET PROJECTIONS* (FISCAL YEAR, BILLIONS OF DOLLARS)

	1987 ACTUAL	1988 BASE	1989	PROJECTIONS 1990	1991	1992	1993
Revenues	854	897	953	1036	1112	1181	1262
Outlays	1005	1055	1129	120	1269	1332	1396
Deficit	150	157	176	167	158	151	134
Debt held by public	1897	2041	2216	2382	2537	2687	2820
			PERCENT OF GNP				
Revenues	19.4	19.2	19.1	19.4	19.5	19.4	19.4
Outlays	22.8	22.5	22.7	22.6	22.3	21.9	21.5
Deficit	3.4	3.4	3.5	3.1	2.8	2.5	2.1
Debt held by public	43	43.6	44.5	44.7	44.6	44.2	43.4

EFFECTS ON CBO BASELINE BUDGET PROJECTIONS OF SELECTED CHANGES IN ECONOMIC ASSUMPTIONS (BILLIONS OF DOLLARS)

	1988	1989	1990	1991	1992	1993
1 percent reduction in real growth, starting January 1988						
Change in deficit	6	21	41	64	90	119
1 percent increase in unemployment rate, starting January 1988						
Change in deficit	24	42	48	55	61	67
1 percent increase in inflation rate, starting January 1988						
Change in deficit	−1	−1	−1	−2	−3	−7
1 percent increase in interest rates, starting January 1988						
Change in deficit	3	11	16	21	26	30

*Congressional Budget Office, *The Economic and Budget Outlook, 1988 Annual Report* (Washington, D.C.: U.S. Government Printing Office, 1988), pp. 50, 63.

Growth is not just a matter of more savings and investment; it also depends on the way the capital is used with labor. There are no signs of a technological slowdown or a reduction in entrepreneurial enterprise in the United States. Yet there are complaints that U.S. firms invest too little in research and development and are too reluctant to undertake projects that require a relatively long time to pay off.

The short planning horizon and high payoffs required by U.S. managers have sometimes been attributed to particular features of U.S. business culture and a dominance of financial motivations over production incentives. There may be something to this characterization but it is also true that there are differences in the incentive structure of the United States and, by contrast, Japan that would not only explain but justify a shorter time horizon.

A difference between this country and Japan that is critical for the choice of a business planning horizon is the interest rate that a business firm faces. The higher the interest rate, the less important is the long-term future because it has to be discounted heavily. Since the real cost of funds in the United States has been two to five times the cost of funds in Japan over the last dozen years or so, U.S. businessmen are only acting rationally when they operate with a shorter planning horizon and insist on relatively high rates of return.

The relatively high cost of funds in the United States is partly the result of the low national savings rate discussed above but partly also the result of features of the U.S. tax system which reduce the after-tax returns to capital. So we are brought again to the federal tax, expenditure, and deficit problem.

THE PROSPECTS FOR SECTORAL CHANGE

Some of the sectoral changes that had been thought to be aspects of long-run trends in the United States have been slowed if not reversed in the last year or so under the influence of the depreciation of the U.S. dollar. In particular, the manufacturing sector has been growing relatively rapidly over the last year, in large part because U.S. industries that were thought to have lost long-run comparative advantage have found that a cheaper dollar makes it possible to export competitively.

There has been a growing interest in the United States in the formulation of an "industrial policy" which is meant to be a set of government programs for the support of particular industries. This type of policy has attracted attention across the political spectrum. There are "conservative" businessmen who believe that they operate at a disadvantage compared to foreign firms that benefit from direct and indirect government subsidies for research, for employee training, for investment, and other business costs. In addition, they see foreign government-sponsored programs for collaborative efforts by their businesses to create new products and break into new markets. There are academics who think that markets do not work efficiently in generating new products and industries. And there are politicians who see their constituents suffer from what they call unfair foreign competition.

In opposition to governmental administration of an industrial policy are conservatives who distrust the potential wisdom and effectiveness of detailed government directives, and liberals who share that distrust. Their argument is that the government lacks the knowledge necessary to decide on the promising sectors and where and how to back them. To the contention that government does, in fact, already interfere through tariffs and other restraints on imports, for example, the response would be that the example demonstrates the lack of judgment that the government displays. There is also little reason to think that there will be a concerted program of industrial investment directed by the government at the sectoral or firm level. It is likely in the future, as in the past, that for the most part, markets will rule.

Predicting new directions for markets is more difficult than setting out the constraints on macroeconomic developments. One major trend that is likely to continue is the internationalization of the U.S. economy. Only a few years ago, in 1977, imports and exports were both about 10 percent of U.S. GNP. In 1987, the shares rose to 11 percent for exports and 15 percent for imports. Currently, however, exports are growing at an annual rate of about 35 percent. As more countries in the world reach levels of technology at which they can become successful suppliers to the U.S. market, it should be expected that the role of imports and exports would increase further, unless the United States becomes more protectionist.

Prediction of the imminence of protectionist policies is essentially a political judgment. Certainly there is more talk about such policies and the recent trade bill provided more opportunities for them. However, the increased recourse to so-called voluntary restraints, negotiated on a bilateral basis between the United States and its trading partners, was a highly protectionist movement. It is not clear that the trade bill is more protectionist.

THE ROLE OF GOVERNMENT IN HIGHER EDUCATION[5]

In considering the future economic setting for higher education the role of government deserves special attention. In 1984 federal, state, and lo-

5. The data in this section are taken from the *Digest of Education Statistics, 1987* (Washington, D.C.: Center for Education Statistics, Office of Educational Research and Improvement, U.S. Department of Education, U.S. Government Printing Office, 1987), p. 228.

cal governments accounted for 44.8 percent of the current-fund revenues of all institutions of higher education in the United States. So there can be no question as to the importance of these sources. As Chart 2.8 indicates, although federal funds have increased in absolute amount over the last ten years, their share of total revenues of institutions of higher education have declined substantially. The importance of state and local contributions has fallen slightly. Tuition, fees, endowment income and other, various private sources have made up the difference.

There are varying reasons for the decline in the role of the different levels of government in financing higher education. Local governments

CHART 2.8. SOURCES OF CURRENT FUND REVENUES OF INSTITUTIONS
OF HIGHER EDUCATION

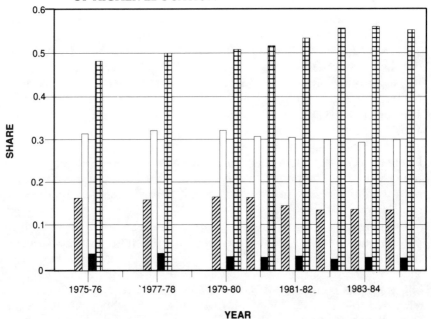

have faced taxpayer "revolts" that have placed limits on their tax revenues. Local funding for elementary and secondary schools went up by 86 percent from 1975 to 1984, but by only 44 percent for institutions of higher education.

The states took over some of the burden that localities were trying to remove. State funding for primary and secondary education slightly more than doubled over the same period as did state funding for higher education. The expansion of state assistance has been, in part, the result of the increasing difficulty of obtaining federal funds.

On the other hand, while federal funding for elementary and secondary education increased by only one third from 1975 to 1984, funding for higher education increased by about 70 percent. The prospects for still another acceleration of federal assistance to higher education are tied up with the federal deficit problem discussed earlier.

An important change that has occurred in the last several years is an increase in federal support for research. The budget of the National Science Foundation which was severely cut in the early years of the Reagan Administration has clearly recovered. It too, however, is subject to the general budgetary constraints, as was evident this year when authorizations had to be tailored to the overall budget limitations.

DEMAND PRESSURES ON HIGHER EDUCATION

Against this overall economic background the next step is to ask whether there are specific implications for higher education, starting with demand factors.

Educators think of education as a process of transferring information and methods of thinking that are important in both the noneconomic as well as the economic functions of an individual. There can be little doubt of the economic importance of higher education in creating useful skills of all types. In addition, as part of its economic role, education serves as a screening mechanism: regardless of what they have learned, persons who successfully negotiate the education system have demonstrated that they have certain talents, useful in the business world, in dealing with institutions, individuals, and problems. We do not know the extent, however, to which individuals can capture for themselves all the benefits of that screening process.

The conventional economic approach to education, which is followed for much of the following discussion, is to think of the demand for higher education, in particular, as generated by individuals and their families, as that is the easiest source of demand to identify. There will be some remarks, however, on the social demand as well.

U.S. RESIDENT DEMANDS

The most fundamental of the demand pressures are demographic: the size of the age cohorts that make up the overwhelming portion of college enrollments. Chart 2.9 shows the number of persons by major racial groups who will reach 18 years of age in each year from 1980 to 2000. With only modest adjustments for immigration and mortality, these people will be the eligible population of college undergraduates. As can be seen, after an uptick next year, there will be substantial decreases in the eligible population of white undergraduates until 1992. By that year the decline will be almost 16 percent from the current level. The numbers of 18-year-old black persons follow roughly the same patterns. The

CHART 2.9. NUMBER OF 18-YEAR-OLD PERSONS IN THE UNITED STATES (THOUSANDS)

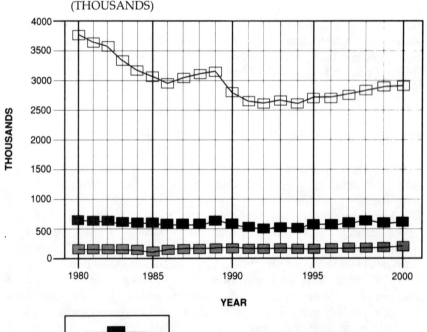

numbers of 18-year-olds in other races have a different pattern, but there are many fewer of them. The overall implication of Chart 2.9 is that pressures for enrollment arising from demographic changes alone will be reduced over the next dozen years.

The next step based on demography is the determination of the proportion of each age cohort that will actually seek entrance to colleges and universities. Table 2.3 provides information on participation rates from 1980 to 1985. As indicated, participation rates for whites, as a fraction of the 18 to 24 age cohorts, have been rising while the rates for blacks and Hispanics have been relatively stable or even falling. Participation rates as a fraction of the high school graduate cohorts have also been rising for whites but have been stable or falling for blacks and Hispanics.

Of the factors determining the rate of participation in higher education, it is clear that disposable income is one of the most important. The rationale and the evidence is reasonably clear, although the exact manner of the interaction deserves further study. As noted above, while average and median family incomes have been rising, median incomes of individuals have been falling. This means that while families are better able to contribute to the costs of a college education, it is at the expense of greater labor effort by family members.

Can family incomes support further tuition increases in the future as they have in the past? As noted, the increase in family incomes has been due more to increased participation of women in the labor force than to increased earnings of individuals. No one knows what the labor force saturation level is, so we do not know if we are close to it. Moreover, the extent of women's participation in the labor force is, itself, a function of the development and financing of child-care facilities. If, however, womens' labor force participation as a source of increased family income does not continue to expand, then families will have more difficulty in meeting tuition increases.

Other influences on the private demand for higher education include the levels of tuition and other costs, the availability and conditions of private and public loan and tuition assistance programs, including interest rates, and the unemployment rates of teenagers.

It became popular among many economists in the 1960s to treat educated persons like any other type of capital asset and the educational process as if it were very much like the process of creating physical capital equipment. This approach, in turn, led to the calculation of rates of return on "investment in human capital," which became, for a time, one of the favorite indoor sports of economists. Though subject to many doubts and criticisms, the activity continues, particularly among those economists who believe they can discern the consequences of reasonably good markets nearly everywhere. Yet, reflecting the controversy

TABLE 2.3. ENROLLMENT RATES IN INSTITUTIONS OF HIGHER EDUCATION BY RACE AND ETHNICITY

YEAR	WHITE		BLACK		HISPANIC	
	18–24	HIGH SCHOOL GRADUATES	18–24	HIGH SCHOOL GRADUATES	18–24	HIGH SCHOOL GRADUATES
1980	26.2	31.8	19.2	27.6	16.1	29.8
1981	26.7	32.5	19.9	28.0	16.7	29.9
1982	27.2	33.1	19.8	28.0	16.8	29.2
1983	27.0	32.9	19.2	27.0	17.2	31.4
1984	28.0	33.7	20.4	27.2	17.9	29.9
1985	28.7	34.4	19.8	26.1	16.9	26.9

that surrounds the concept, there are many different ways to calculate rates of return on education that give different results and contribute to more controversy.

Even if one does not take the rate-of-return calculations at face value, the results do serve the important function of directing attention to economic processes affecting demand for education. A true rate of return is like a price, indicating the net results of the interaction of demand and supply influences. Such a price, in a good market, is both a cause and an effect. It elicits a response and is consistent as a result of the response.

When rate-of-return calculations were first undertaken in the 1960s they seemed on the whole to indicate an acceptable rate of return on a college education. There were some doubts as to the relevance of the results for individual or social decision making but these were generally set aside. Further calculations indicated, again with some controversy, that the rate of return had fallen substantially in the mid-1970s.[6] The most recent calculations show a substantial recovery of the calculated rate of return. The suggestion has been made that this is responsible for the increased rate of participation of 18- to 24-year-old whites, both as a fraction of totals and as a fraction of high school graduates. In contrast, black and Hispanic enrollment ratios have gone down. The calculations present only results and not explanations, and the explanations for the results, if they are significant, are not obvious.

There is no satisfactory way of projecting rates of return on higher education. Even if the evidence on changes in recent rates of return is correct and is taken at face value, and there are many reasons not to do so, it provides no insight into the future. The fall in the rates in the 1970s was not foreseen, nor was the apparent increase in the 1980s.

NONRESIDENTS' DEMANDS FOR U.S. HIGHER EDUCATION

A type of change in demand that seems likely to be accentuated in the future is the growing rate of nonresident students in U.S. colleges and universities. In 1980 these students were 2.4 percent of the total recipients of bachelor's degrees, and 7.5 and 12.8 percent of the recipients of master's and doctor's degrees, respectively. The distribution by field was quite uneven, however, and in engineering the ratio of nonresident students to total degree recipients was 9.3 percent, 27.9 percent, and 37.5 percent for bachelor's, master's, and doctor's degrees, respectively.

6. R. B. Freeman, "The Facts About the Declining Economic Value of College," *Journal of Human Resources* 15 (Winter 1980), pp. 124–142. This article also provides a bibliography that leads to most of the relevant literature.

By 1983, foreign students represented 19.3 percent of total doctorates and 52.9 percent of doctorates in engineering. In 1984, their role had grown still further to 20.9 percent of total doctorates and 54.6 percent of doctorates in engineering. As noted earlier, especially at the doctoral level, participation by U.S. citizens has been declining and their place has been taken by foreign students.

A number of reasons can be cited for the increasing numbers of foreign students in U.S. higher education; not all of these are immediately economic. Examples of noneconomic reasons are the improvement of education standards in developing countries and the teaching of English as a virtually universal language. These developments have increased the accessibility of U.S. higher education to all foreigners. Another factor is less easy to document but, according to many reports, is important: the relative openness of U.S. society.

Economic and political influences are certainly significant, however, as indicated by the changing patterns of enrollment by country of origin. The number of U.S. college and university students in the United States from Iran declined sharply in the 1980s, due to both political and economic factors. Smaller decreases in students from African and Latin American nations have, most likely, been due mainly to economic factors. Marked increases in students from China largely reflect political changes there, but the large increases in numbers from other Asian countries are probably due mainly to economic influences.

Economic growth around the world has increased the ability of both foreign individuals and foreign governments to pay for education in the United States. While educational systems have expanded rapidly at both the primary and secondary levels in both industrialized and developing countries, their systems of graduate education have often not grown at the same rate. This lag may have been for lack of willingness to commit resources in some of the industrialized countries and certainly because of inability to staff graduate programs in many developing countries.

It is possible to create plausible explanations for the increased enrollment of foreign students in graduate education as compared to declining enrollments of U.S. students. Very limited hard information is available, however. It would occur to a calculator of rates of return to education to suggest that the return to the foreign holder of a U.S. Ph.D. in the native country must be higher than the return to a U.S. student here.

All these explanations are likely to be relevant, to different degrees, for different persons and countries. It is likely that they complement explanations in which noneconomic factors, such as the status associated with foreign education, play a role as well. These factors are likely to continue to be important. Income differentials among countries, though they may be reduced, will persist. The trend of the U.S. economy toward becoming more and more open is also likely to persist and that is also likely to increase the attractiveness of U.S. education.

The currently depreciated value of the U.S. dollar has decreased the cost of a U.S. education drastically for residents of other industrialized countries. It would be dangerous to predict that this will continue to be so, though the dollar may well fall still further in the near future. Long-term projections of foreign exchange rates, like long-term projections of other prices, is a particularly tricky business.

SOCIAL DEMANDS FOR EDUCATION

The fact that there are large government subsidies to higher education means either that there is a social demand for education or that the particular persons who benefit from the government subsidies have been especially successful in getting the benefits of the tax and expenditure system for themselves. The latter argument has, in fact, been made. It maintains that tax-financed subsidies are a means of transferring part of the costs of education from the middle- and upper-income groups, who benefit most from these subsidies, to lower-income groups. The conclusion comes from a comparison of the incidence of taxes with the incidence of benefits. The argument gains plausibility from two facts that are relatively easy to establish: first, that state tax systems often have relatively little progressivity, and second, that participation in higher education is correlated with family income.

There are, however, many reasons to believe that there is a social as well as an individual demand for higher education. The subsidies are rationalized on the grounds that increased equality of opportunity is socially desirable. They are also rationalized as a means of student recruitment to educational activities which would otherwise not provide adequate private incentives, but which are regarded as socially important. That is the explanation for federal government support for medical education as well as support for research in colleges and universities.

While there is no reason to believe that these social demands will change, they are made effective through government expenditures, and those are, again, subject to the budgetary constraints discussed above.

SUPPLY CONDITIONS FOR HIGHER EDUCATION

There are, no doubt, important relationships between the aggregate and the sectoral performance of the economy and the financial conditions of higher education. Private gifts go up and down with the stock market and the level of prosperity in the system; a tax and expenditure reform that reduced budget stringency would favor increased support to higher education. Beyond this it is not so clear, and only a few general observations are possible.

The consequences for higher education of changes in the general economic environment depend on the ways in which higher education is provided. Unfortunately we lack a good understanding of the factors determining the "supply" conditions of higher education. There are excellent studies of the level and structure of costs, but, with modest exceptions, these studies do not explain why the costs are what they are. For example, the classic study by Howard Bowen, *The Costs of Higher Education*,[7] traces the trends and documents the differences. The characterization of institutional behavior in this book has been quoted widely and with approval—a testament to its accuracy:

> Each institution raises all the money it can.
>
> Each institution spends all it raises.[8]

However, Bowen does not explain why institutions behave this way; therefore, we cannot really use this characterization to predict how they will behave if the general economic environment should change. Moreover, the quotation implies different kinds of behavior in periods of tight as compared to periods of easy budgets. The quotation implies that in a period of tight budgets the institutions are diligently scrounging for every dollar in order to maintain their establishments. Conversely, the suggestion is that in periods of easy budgets institutions spend freely and do not save and attempt to build endowments.

The depressed state of higher education in England is evidence that, when national budgets are very tight, colleges and universities can lose immunity to cuts. There is no sign of such a degree of tightness yet in the United States. However, if the country slips into the economic stagnation that was identified above as a possible consequence of low savings rates, then higher education, too, would fall on hard times. It is unlikely in this case that donations from private sources would compensate for constraints on government support, because private incomes would also stagnate.

My task here was not to develop a theory of finance and expenditures for higher education. Yet, without a model of some kind, it is not possible to go far in tracing the potential impact of general economic conditions on the financial problems of higher education. The following is an outline of such a model that generates some specific suggestions.

7. Howard Bowen, *The Costs of Higher Education* (San Francisco: The Carnegie Foundation, Jossey-Bass Publishers, 1980).
8. Ibid., p. 20.

The "market" for higher education is not the conventional one for which economists assume, without too much violence to reality, that the supplying "firms" are engaged in various forms of competition to maximize their profits. I suggest, however, that colleges and universities do compete in various ways, though not all compete in the same markets. There are clusters of competing institutions with rather distinct identities, although on the fringes they merge with other clusters. The public and private research universities are one such cluster that is reasonably well defined. It merges at its fringes with other clusters: the universities in which research is a less dominant feature, and the high-standard colleges. These, in turn, merge at their fringes with universities and colleges with less demanding entrance requirements that merge at their fringes with community colleges and junior colleges.

In each cluster—for example, among the research universities—there is "quality competition" that takes a number of different forms: bidding for prestigious faculty members and promising students and vying for research contracts and facilities. This competition requires financial resources, of course, but success itself facilitates the acquisition of those resources.

This quality competition, to some extent, only redistributes the existing educational resources among institutions of higher education. Faculty members with prestigious reputations will move among institutions, but in any short period, the competition will not create more of them. Likewise, the best students may move in waves toward institutions that offer them the most attractive educational packages, but that will not create more well-qualified young people.

Scholarships and other inducements will also make it possible for students to enroll who would not otherwise be able to attend college. And higher faculty salaries will, in some longer run period, attract more capable individuals. These and other improvements can be expected from quality competition.

While quality competition has some valuable social benefits, it is suggested that the rationale for it is, to a considerable extent, the improved access to financial resources that goes along with success. Higher quality is rewarded through research contracts, foundation endowments, alumni gifts, and willingness of student families to pay relatively high tuitions at the private institutions. That is, universities engage in quality competition to improve their access to funds that will permit them to continue to compete.

Further, the competition among the research universities affects other universities and the high-standard colleges because, at their fringes, they are not too different. Institutions in this second group are also engaged in quality competition stressing, perhaps, different elements: teaching, student support, and noncurricular activities, but including enough of the competitive elements of the research universities to be influenced by them. And so the competitive effects go, down to the junior college. Perhaps the most obvious supporting evidence for this assertion, although it is not unequivocal, is that faculty salaries at all institutions move in concert, if not precisely together.

It should immediately be noted, however, that there are cost pressures on higher education institutions in addition to their own quality competition. They are not immune to general inflation. The inflation of salaries of high-level professionals in the private sector provides attractive alternatives for faculty that influence faculty salaries as well. Thus, the increase in costs of higher education is not due only to competition within the education industry.

The distinction between publicly and privately supported institutions is one that cuts across all the clusters. It is not necessary now to document all the differences, but it seems obvious that they affect the nature of the competition and the ability to compete.

This framework, as skeletal as it is, provides at least a partial explanation for the Bowen description of institutional behavior quoted above. The model can also be exploited for some tentative insights into the effects of the kinds of overall trends in the economy as a whole that have been described above. The first question might be this: "How will institutions of higher education react to and determine their sources of finance in the coming years?"

Quality competition for students would not lead to financial problems if the pool of high-quality students with adequate family and federal financing were large enough to fill all the classes of the competing institutions. The most obvious evidence suggesting that this is not the case is the growing share of scholarships and fellowships in total current fund expenditures of institutions of higher education. From 1977 to 1984, this share increased from 8.9 percent to 9.9 percent or by more than 10 percent in seven years.

While one motive for tuition support is to provide opportunities for higher education to students whose families could not otherwise afford it, another motive might be the quality competition described above. Both motives contribute to increases in current expenditures. In any case, private institutions are, in fact, providing more tuition funding, but more of that is based on tuition payments from students. From 1975 to 1984 the share of tuition and fees in total current fund revenues of private institutions of higher education rose from 36.5 percent to 38.7 percent. In the same period tuition and fees at public institutions of higher education rose from 13.0 percent to 14.5 percent of total current fund revenues.

There is a plausible rationale for asking students and their families for higher tuition payments to maintain or improve the quality of their education. It seems less reasonable, however, to put an increasing burden on tuition payers to achieve the social goal of equalizing opportunity.

There is no doubt that higher education in private institutions and higher education in public institutions are substitutes. Whether they are perfect substitutes is a matter of debate not to be entered here. The degree to which the substitution takes place among students and their families will, no doubt, depend in part on relative costs. The reasoning above suggests that, without increased federal programs, the future favors substitution toward state institutions, if the private institutions continue their quality competition. The reasoning also suggests that the private colleges that compete with universities on the fringes will also have increasing financial problems if they try to compete with private universities.

To the extent that there is more federal funding for graduate than for undergraduate education, through research grants as well as scholarship and fellowship programs, the substitution of enrollment in public rather than private institutions will occur more at the undergraduate than at the graduate levels. This would tend to increase the concentration of private universities in graduate education.

On the other hand, if federal support for education increases in the form of tuition support, or in some other form that does not explicitly favor public institutions, the quality competition is also likely to continue. That, in turn, will continue to help push costs upward.

The largest single item of current expenditures by institutions of higher education is for teaching, and faculty salaries are by far the largest single component of teaching costs. The salaries of those faculty who are willing and able to move out of the educational system are more closely tuned to the general economy than are the salaries of faculty without easy substitute employment. It is possible that a pattern characterizing some professional schools might become more common: part-time faculty who value academic employment for the credentialing it provides for nonacademic employment.

In a period of general budgetary stringency it also seems likely that colleges and universities would try to shed their nonteaching functions or fund them from sources that are not closely associated with teaching. It also seems plausible that there would be a reconsideration of the pattern of general support for higher education, irrespective of the nationality of the students.

Very much depends on the evolution of national attitudes toward higher education and its various functions; and in this, the role of our national leadership is critical.

CONCLUSIONS

This is a time of more than usual uncertainty with respect to future economic trends. It is certain that future economic conditions will be of great importance for the demand for higher education and for the conditions of its supply. Continued growth with continued decline in median incomes will cut into the ability of individuals to meet the costs of higher education. Continued growth which results in higher median incomes and larger government contributions to the costs would have quite different consequences.

The increase in costs in higher education that have been experienced may be the result, in part, of the quality competition that exists at many levels. This competition, though contributing to maintenance and improvement of educational excellence may, to some extent, simply redistribute existing educational resources rather than increase them or improve educational performance.

Without an increase in federal educational assistance programs, state institutions of higher education can be expected to do better than private institutions in the quality competition. At the university level, the latter may come to specialize increasingly in graduate education.

There is considerable inertia in the structure and substance of higher education, as is true for many other social institutions. Yet there is currently a sense of crisis in higher education, a feeling that past patterns are breaking and the future must be and will be different. Demographic changes in the eligible student population and among faculties, changes in the U.S. economy, changes in educational financing, and, perhaps, changes in educational methods and substance are all contributing to this mood. Only a few of the sources and potential consequences of these changes have been highlighted in this chapter. It is clear that there is a substantial agenda for research that will help in making policy for the new environment that is emerging.

3

HIGHER EDUCATION IN A CHANGING ENVIRONMENT: SOME SCHOLARLY AND ECONOMIC IMPERATIVES

HAROLD T. SHAPIRO

It seems to be the opinion of many in higher education that their opportunities and, therefore, their actions are increasingly shaped by rapid changes in various dimensions (e.g., scientific, technological, moral, aesthetic) of the national and international environment. In particular, there is a growing interest regarding the potential impact on higher education of the changing economic environment developing at both the national and international levels. For American colleges and universities, however, novelty and change by themselves are not new visitors. Selective adaptation to change has been an important characteristic of American higher education, especially in the years since World War II. For example, institutions of higher education have adapted—more or less successfully—to significant changes in:

- the age profile of the population and the faculty
- the distribution of enrollment between public and private institutions
- the priorities of various external funding sources
- the importance of federal government finance
- the geographic distribution of students and institutions
- the spectrum of scientific and scholarly opportunities
- the nature and extent of public regulations
- the public attitude toward higher education

All this has been accomplished by ostensibly conservative institutions during an era of unprecedented change in the world of scholarship and during alternating periods of economic expansion (mostly) and economic recession. In the last decades, therefore, American institutions of higher education have accumulated experience with expansion, change, limits, and shifting expectations. Indeed, universities and academic disciplines have proved to be rather open systems. Although adaptation to change is not a new trial for American higher education, the coming years are expected to bring a new set of issues to test our adaptability, and that is the focus of this chapter.

It is certainly clear that economic forces will continue to influence the evolution of higher education in many ways—through both macro and industry-specific effects. For example, growth in real family incomes and the capacity of federal, state, and local governments—through direct budget appropriations or tax expenditures—to support existing and/or new initiatives in higher education will remain important parameters governing the options available to faculty and university and college administrators. My own view (forecast) is that we can expect little growth in subsidies to higher education from either federal or state governments, and that the latter are increasingly likely also to restrain growth in tuition revenues. I will focus my attention, however, on the economic impact of certain intellectual developments—changes within the academy, so to speak—and on the capacity of leading colleges and universities to accommodate these developments *within existing* institutional forms and commitments.

When I speak of the existing institutional forms and commitments of leading colleges and universities, I refer in particular to the commitment of contemporary colleges and universities to both education and scholarship and to a design of these institutions—including their disciplinary focus—that reflects their joint responsibility to teaching, research, and, for many, advanced research training. The issue will be whether the scholarly and economic imperatives to be faced in the coming decades will continue to allow this particular sector of higher education to accept responsibility not only for teaching (preserving, transmitting, and remembering), but also for a serious commitment to scholarship (evaluation, criticism, and renovation). Strains are already visible. For example, it can be effectively argued that trends in contemporary scholarship and their associated economic imperatives are placing new burdens on the capacity of leading American colleges and universities to buffer the various disciplines from the changing priorities and demands of their various patrons. In such an environment, it may prove more difficult for universities—as currently designed—to meet their responsibilities to the world of scholarship.

Indeed, we should remind ourselves that academic freedom itself, now one of the bedrocks of American higher education, is historically a rather peculiar and relatively recent development. In the modern world, society's support for academic freedom can probably be sustained only when a nation possesses faith in knowledge and a certain degree of self-confidence. While academic freedom may have been tolerated originally because political rulers thought university activities irrelevant, the work of the contemporary university is inextricably tied to many essential aspects of modern life and is of direct interest to society as a whole. If, for economic and cultural reasons, our society should feel incapable of sustaining a position of leadership in the next decades, academic freedom may find itself increasingly besieged. For this and many other reasons the evolution of higher education in America will be tied in important ways to the overall health of the U.S. economy.

THE CURRENT ENVIRONMENT

Although colleges and universities have demonstrated a remarkable capacity to change, at any moment in time there is an inventory of symptoms reflecting the imperfect and incomplete nature of this adjustment process. I would like to highlight some of the current symptoms of these various ongoing strains—most of which are well known—and then consider certain aspects of contemporary developments in scholarship, their resource implications for individual colleges and universities, and some of the potential repercussions these matters may have on the evolution of higher education. Consider the following inventory.

1.   A chronic perceived shortage of resources, even when funding seems generous by historical standards.

2.   The growing public concern regarding both the cost and price of higher education despite an apparently low price elasticity of demand for entrance to leading colleges and universities. Higher education continues to exhibit a tenacious preference for a high-cost structure in the belief—perhaps mistaken—that given its spectrum of responsibilities no better alternatives to quality are available.

3.   A perceived increase in the unpredictability of the resource flow that sustains both education and scholarship. This new level of uncertainty has, of course, a direct impact on the scholarly agenda and other aspects of the communal life and responsibilities of individual colleges and universities.

4.   Endless discussions regarding the inability of specialized "discipline-based" scholars to work with colleagues in their own departments, let alone across the disciplines. There is an associated anxiety regarding the capacity of colleges and universities to meet the need for

depth and clarity of understanding so characteristic of disciplinary based scholarship and learning and the growing interdisciplinary needs of both education and scholarship. This is but one example of the continuing concern regarding the impact of various centrifugal forces pulling the university away from both its essential disciplinary core and its sense of community.

5.   Increasing concern regarding the ability of faculties to mobilize themselves to meet (interest themselves in meeting) their joint obligations to undergraduate teaching. There is growing apprehension that the competitive demands of specialized scholarship and other developments have placed an irreparable rift between graduate and undergraduate education and may have impaired the capacity of leading colleges and universities both to remain centers of modern scholarship and to fulfill their broader educational functions. For example, the shorter and shorter time frame between developments in basic research and the incorporation of these new ideas into marketable products is a new environmental factor creating new strains as well as new opportunities. This development has increased the interaction of faculty with external communities in ways that may have expanded the resource base, but may have also impacted both the scholarly agenda and the focus of interest on education versus research and development.

6.   Increasing difficulty in finding any agreement on the procedures, methods, and standards of evaluation by which to choose among alternative points of view in the humanities and some of the social sciences. Some go so far as to say that there is no way to define, let alone recognize, either competence or incompetence. Within the humanities—especially within literature—it seems harder now to speak of truth and understanding; one speaks, more simply, of one's perspective. We are more concerned than ever about whether it is possible to read old books without adopting old loyalties. My own view is that the newer approaches to humanistic studies clarify a great deal even as they make interpretation and meaning more complex. These same developments, however, have led to some general apprehension about whether there are or should be any nonarbitrary, nonpolitical methods of selecting an undergraduate curriculum in this general area. This is much more than a disciplinary issue, since these departments have been left with much of the task—within the undergraduate curriculum—of dealing not only with our understanding of civilization, but with our responsibility for transmitting those aspects of the humanist tradition that deal with understanding, judging, and articulating meaning.

7.   Growing concern by some publics in "what is going on" on the nation's campuses. There is an apparent willingness to support ever-rising

costs, but higher education is facing increasing calls for accountability regarding issues such as efficiency and access. Furthermore, there seems to be a growing public anxiety regarding both the nature and implication of the scientific research within the university and the nature of higher education's responsibilities for student's ethical and moral development and commitments. In addition, there are ever-increasing demands to put new social action items on higher education's agenda. All this may reflect some loss of confidence in the value of knowledge, in the power of reason, and in the aspirations of faculty and university administrators. Although academic communities talk of a new curriculum, many among the public seem to be seeking a new spirit and a different set of commitments.

8.   Astonishingly poor general literacy in science. The almost total lack among a distressingly high proportion of college graduates of any real understanding of the nature, promise, and limitations of modern science fuels the "anti-science" campaigns and threatens to undermine a good deal of important public policy. In addition, we have failed to attract enough students to science and engineering to meet the national need.

9.   Failures of higher education—and other current social arrangements—to increase the participation of underrepresented minorities in higher education.

THE "ECONOMICS" OF CURRENT INTELLECTUAL DEVELOPMENTS

These apprehensions have many and varied sources, but it is useful to ponder some of the additional and less well publicized developments in scholarship (the scholarly imperatives) that are helping to produce these symptoms. Conceivably, an increased sensitivity to these will help us engage in the process of thoughtful and selective change that has always been the key to the continued vitality of leading colleges and universities. Consider the following contemporary developments.

1.   Advances in scientific instrumentation have led to *qualitative* changes in the scholarly agenda. This change has enabled us to look at old challenges in a new way as well as to perceive new challenges. In general, these changes have increased the cost and complexity of scholarly investigations in all disciplines, from anthropology, biology, and classics to language study and zoology. These changes in the scholarly agenda, however, contain within them a specific economic imperative as they require us to associate a lot more capital (facilities, equipment,

technical support, etc.) with each student, each scholar, and each teacher, if they are to operate at the scholarly and educational frontiers. Thus, many contemporary intellectual imperatives have associated with them a demanding economic imperative. Higher education, in short, is becoming much more capital intensive. This together with increased specialization is making the cost of faculty turnover, particularly in science and engineering, very daunting indeed.

2. The availability of vast new levels of computational power—at ever-declining prices "per cycle"—has also changed the way we approach the scholarly agenda and the scholarly agenda itself. Indeed, the decreasing per unit cost of computation has been outpaced by the rapidly increasing demand for "units." Now a whole new information transport infrastructure is needed. This development has also increased the level of capital required to support each member of the university community. The new information and communication world made possible by new technology has created the potential for a new scholarly environment, but at dramatically increased cost. Productivity gains, *if any*, have been taken in quality improvement and agenda expansion rather than cost reduction.

3. An incipient revolution in the production, distribution, and pricing of information—the very foundation of higher education—also threatens to raise the cost to colleges and universities of data acquisition. These changes are not widely understood or fully appreciated. They may restructure the framework within which scholarship is performed and financed. This development has also created many uncertainties, and uncertainty always raises costs and postpones needed adjustments. We are uncertain what form the future research library might take. We are uncertain how national telecommunication policies in various countries will influence international scholarship. We are uncertain regarding the importance of consortial activities designed to expand access to information resources. We are uncertain how our own federal information policies will affect university costs and operations.

4. There is a growing necessity to study complex systems which require interdisciplinary work. For example, there is increasing scholarly interest in the global environment, in health, in ecology, and in international trade. Furthermore, we see increased interest across such fields as protein chemistry and biology, cognitive studies and language acquisition, literature and law, science and sociological knowledge, chemistry and materials science. This need for interdisciplinary study places pressure on both the existing organization of colleges and universities, and on existing methods of jointly financing undergraduate education, graduate education, and scholarship. As a result, there are serious discus-

sions of the possible need for changes in the way universities play their role in the production and distribution of knowledge. For example, should research institutes replace graduate programs? Should the disciplinary organization of universities be strengthened, reshaped, or retained? Can disciplines (and scholars) retain their intellectual integrity and respond effectively to new interdisciplinary demands?

The critical fact that so many of these new developments require more resources per student and more resources per faculty member to function on the frontier of knowledge has a number of important implications, including the following.

1. A great many institutions find themselves with a large number of underfinanced efforts and without an effective mechanism to adjust by setting priorities in a collegial yet more decisive fashion. This dilemma is a serious threat to the quality of higher education. We may not be able to generate the resources, institution by institution, to carry forward the full complement of existing activities at the same level of quality.

2. In many areas, tenure and library access are no longer enough to pursue an effective career. Continued access to external research funds—always relatively unpredictable—is also required. In such circumstances it is more difficult to develop an independent scholarly agenda, and a part of the connection between tenure and academic freedom is somewhat undermined. In addition, external funding sources often take little responsibility for education.

3. In many areas these same developments also require an increase in the number of graduate students, post-doctoral students, research assistants, and technical support staff per scholar. This can change the balance of activities and interests in the university in significant ways and raise the level of support costs for each faculty-investigator.

The biggest issue of all, however, relates to the meaning of these changes for the relationship between scholarly commitments and undergraduate education, and in some people's minds, between our obligations to research and our responsibility for graduate education. One increasingly hears from faculty that they really prefer post-doctoral students to graduate research assistants because this arrangement is so much more efficient. Thus, the tension between teaching and research obligations extends beyond undergraduate concerns.

Could it be that university roles in research and undergraduate education have diverged too far? Could it be that undergraduate education "gets in the way" of front-line research? Could it be that the increasingly specialized focus of scholarly commitments is at odds with the necessity of faculty to work as a community in their responsibility for undergraduate education? Perhaps the gulf between the needs of undergraduate and graduate education is now too wide and this might explain why so few undergraduates pursue graduate studies. Do we need to consider new faculty career patterns that would allow alternating periods of focus on teaching and scholarship? Should we keep the research and education enterprises together? There is, after all, some significant difference between learning science and doing science—particularly when so much of the research agenda is externally driven. It is important to understand what kinds of distortions of university priorities, if any, are created by "blockbuster grants" (e.g., SDI, AIDS, "centers"). All these externally funded initiatives require some type of cost-sharing and thus "dictate" the allocation of internal funds. Do these externally funded research-oriented "centers" also drive the system away from undergraduate education?

In addition, we have the following environmental factors placing more upward pressure on cost structures.

1.   There is an increasing demand for student support services—a new paternalism driven by many factors, including the increasing heterogeneity of the student body and a growing proportion of foreign students—and a lack of consensus about the scope of individual and family versus institutional responsibility. The growing professionalization, vocationalization, diversification, secularization, and specialization of the academic community have brought about, in addition to many benefits, a certain loss of coherence and personal meaning. In any case, these new demands add to the economic imperatives' increasing costs.

2.   The possible elimination of mandatory retirement is seen by some to threaten, forestall, and/or make more expensive important aspects of an institution's capacity for self-renewal.

3.   The increasing cost of responding to the complexities of government regulation provides yet further amplitude to the wave of forces increasing costs.

4.   We face a declining youth population with an increasing at-risk segment just as demand for well-trained employees will be rising. Some of the fastest growing cohorts of our population are opting out of advanced education, particularly in science. Although the particulars differ by discipline, within higher education there are too few scholars in the pipeline gaining the most advanced training. Economy-wide, there is an overall projected shortage of scientists and engineers, and for higher education, at least a temporary shortfall of talented Ph.D.'s in the humanities. Given the steadily growing demand—economy-wide—for people with advanced training, these factors should serve to increase faculty salaries at rates considerably in excess of other wage rates. Fi-

nally, market competition is increasing the disparity of faculty salaries among the disciplines, generating further tensions in a community where all are valued and where all must focus together on undergraduate education. In this area, therefore, we have a market development that increases both costs and concerns for community-wide issues.

Thus, from a wide variety of sources, intellectual and economic, forces are emerging that are raising the cost structures of existing institutions of higher education. Indeed, there seems little alternative to these rising costs if we are to operate on the frontier of scholarship and education and within existing institutional commitments and forms. In addition to incorporating these new costs, it is essential that we increase the overall participation of currently underrepresented minorities in higher education.

All these needs must confront the knowledge that there is some limit to the proportion of the nation's GNP that can be devoted to higher education. Higher education may be priced below actual cost and still not be affordable! In other words, the economy may not be able to support the rising cost structures of existing institutional forms and commitments. We should recall that, although we spend more of our GNP on higher education than other countries—and have a wide variety of unique achievements—we do not always sense a benefit corresponding to the extra investment. In any case, if we are extremely lucky the country will experience a sustained and an unusually rapid pace of economic growth and these looming "bills" can be financed by a part of the national growth dividend. It seems to me, however, that we cannot rely on such an easy solution to the challenge ahead of us. Instead, some combination of the following steps will prove necessary to resolve both the intellectual and the economic imperatives before higher education:

1. serious attention to the enhancement of productivity in higher education. Our society may not continue to tolerate such a high-cost producer of information and there may be better alternatives to existing forms and practices for the generation, organization, and transmission of knowledge;

2. new and imaginative approaches to the setting of priorities that will allow or even encourage institutions to pursue a more selective course. It is our responsibility to examine this particular course in any case. We have barely begun to use the power of new technology or new research findings on learning in our educational programs. Our teaching paradigms have shown the greatest resistance to change—even as we participate in revolutionary changes in the world of scholarship.

Unfortunately, neither of these approaches has characterized the last decade. Let us hope we can do better in the decade ahead.

SECTION II
COMMENTARIES

DEREK BOK

Harvard University

Let me begin by commenting briefly on each of the three chapters in the
preceding section. With respect to Mr. Lindsey's chapter, I do not feel
that my master's degree in economics from George Washington quali-
fies me to respond to his economic analysis in tones other than rever-
ence and respect. With regard to education, I agree with him that in all
probability there will be a great unwillingness to raise taxes in the next
few years and that the government deficit is going to keep public support from rising. As a result, there will be pressure to close the kinds of
gaps, benefits, and loopholes that higher education depends on substantially, and that will be very difficult. Nevertheless, I would question
much of the rest of what he said about the implications of future economic trends for higher education.

To begin with, I think that the society is going to become more complex and jobs will become more demanding, whether we are more statist, in his terms, or more individualistic. As a result, the demand for
better education to meet a more difficult and demanding world will increase regardless of which way the ideological pendulum swings. In
other words, I disagree with the connection Lindsey draws between individualism and education.

I would acknowledge that there may be some increase in consumerism among students and their parents, but I do not believe that these
consumers will behave as Lindsey suggests. In his view, students and
their parents get more power in an individualistic world; as a result, the
need or demand for a liberal arts education will be greater. Now it is
conceivable that the liberal arts do prepare people to be more imaginative and to cope better in this kind of a world. We often say so. I am
not sure, however, that students necessarily believe this or that they are
going to demand more liberal arts education. Rather, it is more likely
that they will press for greater vocationalism in education. Further, I
do not believe that students will become more demanding, as Lindsey
suggests, just because they are paying a larger share of their education
costs. Students in private universities have paid a good deal more for
their education than students in public universities for a long time. But it
would be very difficult to substantiate the notion that students in private
universities have been more demanding or have exerted more pressure

on the quality and nature of their education than have their counterparts in public universities. And I doubt that this will change in the future. I also do not think that students will press hard for better teaching just because they pay more for their education. I see no historical evidence to support this view.

Although I may regret it, I believe that students at COFHE (Consortium on Financing Higher Education) institutions are principally motivated by the academic reputation of their universities. I even suspect that this is more important to students in choosing a university than the nature of the education that is actually provided. Hence, as the competition for jobs and good careers increases, I would look for more pressure to get into the reputedly best universities and not much pressure to change the nature of undergraduate teaching. Hence, although I would prefer it to be otherwise, I fear that consumer pressures will neither bring about more liberal arts education nor force us to change the quality of education. Instead, in the future as in the past, we will have to improve liberal arts programs and the quality of education by summoning our own internal motivations and not because students have forced us to do so.

In the second chapter, Professor Eckaus very wisely remained within the ramparts of economics, and I would not dream of trying to pursue him into that well-defended redoubt. From the standpoint of COFHE institutions, however, the most important statement he made is at the very end of his chapter where he asserts that private colleges and universities will gradually lose out to public colleges and universities in the quality competition if federal support does not increase. Since the likelihood that federal support will increase is rather dim, all of us who represent private institutions should be concerned with his prediction. We will all suffer if it is correct. Nevertheless, I doubt that matters are quite as simple as his model makes out.

This is a point that I would make about almost everything I have read in these three chapters. Briefly put, I would be wary of applying economic models to the future of higher education. There are simply too many variables that are left out. In particular, such models tend to overlook the ability and resourcefulness of private universities to do a lot of things—to find more gifts, to seek out more sources of income generally, to save money on scholarships if need be, to find more older or foreign students, or to do a number of other things that we cannot even anticipate. Private universities are very resourceful institutions and will work very hard to keep from losing quality, even if federal student support does not increase. Their welfare also depends not only on the volume of federal support but on the forms in which it is given. Certainly, in the case of federal student aid, much depends not only on how much federal student aid increases but on how much it is allowed to offset the higher tuitions that students pay to attend private universities.

Let me close this criticism with a private example of my own, as I look at the experience of Harvard University over the last 15 years. These were years in which the student population declined substantially, in which SAT scores on the whole declined significantly, in which there was a very rapidly widening gap between Ivy League tuitions and public university tuitions. In light of these trends, simple models would have predicted 15 years ago that institutions like mine were going to lose badly in the coming competition for students. In fact, however, we experienced significant increases in applications; we witnessed a decline in the loss of applications from my institution to public universities over that period; we suffered no decline in SAT scores; and saw a 30 percent increase in merit scholars. In short, abstract, simple models are going to have to be considerably more sophisticated than they are now if they are going to do a good job of predicting what will happen to us.

In Harold Shapiro's chapter, he discussed a number of interesting trends and projections. Certainly there is much in his analysis that suggests that the economic imperatives are all moving in the direction of higher costs and there is much to suggest that the fiscal environment is getting tougher. In other words, we should all be discouraged about the future. Nevertheless, looking back over the history of higher education, we can point to many past predictions about how impossible it would become for society to sustain private universities or what the demographic downturn would do to higher education. Most of these predictions did not come true. As a result, although the projections we have heard should undoubtedly give us food for thought, it would be premature to become discouraged. If we are resourceful enough, there will be many ways for us to adapt and many unanticipated events that may change the picture. In the end, perhaps our greatest protection lies in our growing importance to the society that sustains us. So long as this trend continues, society may find it more difficult, rather than less, to allow our institutions to decline in quality.

WILLIAM MASSY

Stanford University

Harold Shapiro and I were in a meeting in September, 1988 when somebody said, "We're digging up snakes faster than we can kill them." I have the feeling we're doing that with all the different views being expressed in these essays, but that's the fun of diversity.

In responding to the chapters in the first section, I have organized my thoughts around the "supply and demand model." My comments first address the demand side and then deal with the capacity of institutions to deliver on the demand.

There are some negatives in the demand picture, discussed in all three chapters. Most of them are obvious. The supply of 18-year-olds is projected to dip until 1992, and then rise slowly. However, I don't think that this is a big factor for most of our institutions, certainly not for the selective ones. More seriously, there are barriers to rising participation rates for minorities. I disagree with the notion that participation rates for minorities are dropping because of a calculation or judgment that the rate of return for higher education is dropping. I don't think so. The problem is the constraints on their flow into the higher education system—the K through 12 problem—rather than any lack of economic return if they can get in and be successful. We have to do something about all of that.

The biggest problem on the demand side is the problem of affordability. As a friend of mine on the economics faculty at Stanford said recently, "The problem is that higher education is underpriced all right, but it's not affordable." Certainly people perceive that to be the case, and I think there's enough truth to it that we have to pay attention.

First, there is a fundamental problem due to the intensity of quality competition among institutions. In my judgment that does drive costs up. There is no reason that a college or university cannot get along with price increases at 2 percent real or so, or even less if it has to. The problem is that we don't want to, and the reason we don't want to is that we want to improve ourselves. We don't have to hold price down because the demand elasticity is low enough that people somehow will pay the higher price. Higher prices result from quality incentives and the inelasticity of demand.

The private research universities are the price leaders for tuition, and I think we have to ask ourselves which way the cross-subsidy is now going. For many years, the conventional wisdom on our campuses has been that research subsidizes undergraduate education because of indirect cost recovery. But is this true? I was recently on an AAU committee that looked at indirect cost recovery, and I came away convinced that, if anything, the subsidy is the other way around. There's no doubt that research contributes to the cost of graduate education (they're joint products, in fact), but when we look at the capital that's going into research and the kinds of demands that are being placed on us for cost-sharing, there is a very real question of whether research is in fact being subsidized by undergraduate education.

If such a subsidy exists, it is another factor pushing tuition rates up. And since the private research universities provide a price umbrella for all, such a subsidy also aids research and scholarship—quality generally—in universities and colleges without heavy research programs. Whether that's good or not depends on one's point of view, or rather which demand function you happen to be concerned with. In any case, however, there's no doubt that the federal budget situation is going to exacerbate the problem by placing even greater pressure on research universities to cross-subsidize sponsored programs from all available sources. I think that's going to be true for the next decade. Beyond that, who knows? It would be nice if it ends earlier, but I don't think it will.

There are some positives on the demand side as well. Participation rates are trending up for majority students—that is, for people who do not face those artificial constraints. I agree with Larry Lindsey that higher education's ship is coming in sociologically and philosophically. Empowerment of the individual is proceeding apace, and whether or not one cares to call it economic individualism, the result is that we are perceived as being more and more valuable. I can't agree with all of Lindsey's mechanism, but there's no doubt that individual empowerment and education are complements. This is true both for professional and vocational education and—more profoundly—for the liberal arts. So we have what in marketing is called a "rising market." The question is what we can do with that market.

We're also in a strong market internationally. Dick Eckaus said that foreign students are now 10 to 15 percent of the enrollment. I've seen another estimate that there are now 350,000 foreign students in higher education here, and that the figure is expected to go to a million by the year 2000. Suppose the average expenditure of a foreign student in the United States is $10,000 to $15,000, considering they have to live here, pay tuition, and so on. This comes to three to six billion dollars of foreign exchange now, and 10 to 15 billion dollars in the year 2000—which is a lot of money. We don't give financial aid to foreign students at anywhere near the rates we do for domestic students, so most of this money comes from abroad—money we badly need. And because the marginal costs are low relative to the marginal revenue for these students, we probably make money on them at the margin. So the international sector is another element of our growth market.

Finally, research funding is still a high priority because of what people perceive it can do for our international economic competitiveness, military security, and regional economic development (although that's easily overstated). This is true of training as well as research. So, lots of people think we're important: the potential is there, the positives outweigh the negatives.

Taking all these factors together, there is reason to believe that the 1990s will be a period of strong demand. The question is how we deal with the demand—whether we use it to move to a position of greater strength, or whether we end up at the end of the 1990s in a position of relative weakness because we failed to serve the demand in some way or another. Assuming we do adapt, do we do it in a way that continues the important role universities and colleges have played in providing intellectual leadership rather than simply responding to their customers? Lots of institutions in our society are adept at responding to their customers; you see them all around. But colleges and universities are supposed to beat their own drums and march to those drums. We have to find a way to do that without ignoring the very real pressures on the demand side. The intellectual challenge is how to maintain ourselves as the guardians of important social and intellectual values, and at the same time adapt appropriately to the demands of those who pay for our services.

Now for the supply side, beginning with a few comments on the impact of the economy on colleges and universities. To paraphrase a recent statement by Stanford economist Lee Bach, for the period into the mid-1990s, the most likely scenario is that "it's going to be a very nice time." That is to say, the economy looks good, it looks strong, it looks solid, though there will not be a ranging boom. That was the consensus of a group of faculty from our economics department and the Hoover Institution—not all Republicans, let me assure you. The general feeling was that things are in reasonably good shape, but that we are in a tense period in which policy errors are not unlikely and such errors could lead to major problems. If we stay on the rails everything will be smooth, but if we go off the rails it's a long way down. And it could be down in either direction—recession or inflation—though if we do go off the rails, I think inflation is the greater worry.

The reason we have more to fear from inflation is that the underlying causes of inflation are rather popular politically, even though we don't like the outcome. As Larry Lindsey noted, Machiavelli was right in saying that one accomplishes certain goals by debasing the currency.

In our case that means easy money and providing more resources for the disadvantaged and even the middle class—people who feel that they have a claim. If Machiavelli really were in charge of the Fed, he might wait quietly until the deficit were under control (so there would be no need to keep borrowing new money), then very slowly and carefully take the national debt out long, and then let the dollar dive! "Good heavens," he would say to those who hold our debt, "I'm sorry about that. It'll never happen again." And of course, in the meantime the real value of that debt would have gone down by half. He wouldn't be able to borrow new money or refund very soon because it would take a while to restore confidence—but in a decade all would be forgotten.

The big question, of course, is whether the rest of the world, and particularly the Japanese, will continue to lend to us at reasonable interest and exchange rates. Do they wonder if Machiavelli might live here? Or maybe that the same thing might happen by indirection? There is no assurance that they'll keep lending to us on current terms. In 1987, suddenly $100 billion of our investment from abroad came from central banks, and $60 billion was all there was from the voluntary sector. The voluntary sector is back in 1988, but it's very volatile and things are finely balanced. It wouldn't take much, I think, to cause a panic that would force us to some combination of high interest rates and a devalued dollar.

High interest rates represent one of a number of factors that could trigger a recession. Others include the savings and loan and Latin American debt situations that could cause liquidity problems. And any kind of economic downturn, especially coupled with high interest rates, could cause all that corporate leverage to come home to roost in the form of bankruptcies and more unemployment.

It's also possible that we could have stagflation. Imagine a situation where the dollar goes down (making imports cost more) and exports go up causing sectoral bottlenecks and thus cost-push inflation. The Fed drives up interest rates to the point that the economy goes into recession but we still have bottlenecks.

As far as colleges and universities are concerned, all these dire possibilities mean that we have to plan our strategy carefully. We should develop contingency plans for each of the alternatives. I happen to think that inflation is more likely to be a problem, so Stanford is geared to handle that more than recession, but we need to worry about both scenarios.

The other potential impact of the general economy on higher education is new taxes, more particularly taxes on colleges and universities. I took Larry Lindsey's suggestion that higher education might be taxed on a for-profit basis, and I ran Stanford's numbers through the model. Starting with operating revenue from our published financial statements, I subtracted current expense to get an "operating margin" of $24 million. Subtracting historical cost depreciation of $60 million leaves $180 million, which brings us to the question of gifts. Many of the gifts we get now are gifts to capital—that is, to endowment or plant. I didn't look up the exact number but the fraction of gifts for capital is well over 50 percent, quite possibly two-thirds or so. Well, is that operating income? No, it's more like going to the stock market to raise equity capital. Should it be taxed? Absolutely not! Taxing a corporation's issuance of stock would be a crazy thing to do, especially in a world where capital formation is a big problem. If the government taxed gifts as current income, as I think it would be tempted to do, capital formation for colleges and universities would be a gigantic problem. Where could one draw the line to determine what is a gift for operations and what is a gift that is or could be for capital? And all this is complicated by the fact that depreciation schedules are based on historical costs which lag behind replacement costs. (For Stanford, by the way, the difference is $93 million versus $60 million.) And even replacement cost depreciation lags behind what it actually costs to create science facilities of ever greater complexity, pay for it up front, and then recover over time via the overhead rates. The kind of taxation that Dick Eckaus was talking about would be of very great concern. So, I'm not at all sure that becoming for-profit is the answer although doing a careful multi-institutional analysis might not be a bad idea.

Finally, here are a couple of thoughts on capital. There is a shortage of capital in the United States and worldwide. This comes at a time when colleges and universities are becoming capital intensive. Certainly that's true of the research universities, where the increasing complexity of facilities and equipment is very much in evidence. The quality competition Dick Eckaus referred to is also driving the need for capital, since faculty recruitment and retention depend on having state-of-the-art laboratories and computers. A Stanford trustee remarked when we sought approval of yet another fume-hood exhaust project (to raise the stacks 30 feet over the rooflines to avoid air reentrainment problems), "Oh, I see we're becoming a smokestack industry." Walk around our campus, you see its true; sometimes it doesn't smell so good, either.

Furthermore, information technology is making capital investment in all academic areas worthwhile; the opportunities are not just in the hard sciences. We now can do fascinating things in libraries that we couldn't do before. The same is true for the liberal arts and social sciences. But, as others have said, it's noteworthy that the organizational dynamics of higher education cause the fruits of these capital investments to be taken out mainly as quality increases rather than unit cost decreases—where the definition of quality is determined mostly by consumers. That is appropriate to the extent that we're supposed to march to our own drummer. But the public may be getting tired of paying for ever-increasing "quality"; that's what the flack in the public media is all about.

While better facilities and equipment benefit faculty, the idea that we must finance them from current operations rather than gifts and debt is not widely accepted. The need for investment comes at a time of capital shortage. It is getting harder to borrow the capital that we need because real interest rates are high. Gifts for facilities are very difficult to raise, and the internal generation of capital is tough for several reasons. First, the culture of higher education does not lend itself to setting aside large amounts of current revenue, including current gifts, for transfers to plant. There is great pressure to spend, because of the high subjective discount rate for what we do later as opposed to what we do now. Second, we have not been depreciating our assets on our financial statements. The Financial Accounting Standards Board may change that, and I want to say that I support that change. That position has been unpopular with some of my colleagues, but I'm convinced it's a step in the right direction. We should start putting depreciation front and center. My only regret is that the provision for depreciation will be based on historical cost rather than replacement cost. But historical cost depreciation is a start, and it will help drive home the point that we need to provide cash flow for capital renewal from our own operations.

When we do achieve operating surpluses, or even show substantial nonmandatory transfers from operating income, the cry comes up, "Ah ha, you really are for-profit. We knew it all the time. You just want to amass financial resources." When we answer by talking about the need for capital, we seem defensive. But it's still true, in my opinion. And that leads to the need that Dick Eckaus stressed—the need for a better theory of finance and expenditure for higher education. I think it is an urgent need, because much of the foolishness that arises when one talks about the economics of higher education results from lack of a good theory. People take what they know about for-profit enterprises and transfer it over uncritically, producing false conclusions. There also has been a stream of academic research that holds that a university is a faculty-labor cooperative. Indeed, there's some truth to that, but the term carries the connotation that what we do is really for private rather than public benefit—that is, for the benefit of the participants, who may take it out in nonmonetary ways by being able to further their career goals, have a good life, go to conferences, and so on. In the political arena this reinforces the feeling that there's something wrong with colleges and universities, especially the elite ones, which undermines our support on key economic and policy decisions.

The fact of the matter is that colleges and universities do maximize a subjectively determined "utility function," subject to production, market, and financial constraints. Our production and market demand functions do not differ in principle from those of for-profit enterprises. The financial constraint requires that, on average over time, revenues have got to equal or exceed expenses. If they don't the institutions will have to contract or even disappear. The essential difference between the theory of the profit-making firm and the nonprofit enterprise is that for the latter the "profit function" is a constraint rather than the objective. As a result, the real action comes in determining the institution's utility function. Who should determine it? Who does determine it? How does it change over time? We cannot predict how colleges and universities will react to different economic circumstances until we know something about their utility functions.

As Derek Bok commented, the questions are extraordinarily complicated, and simple models do not work. I have to differ with him, though, in that I don't think we can afford to be pessimistic about our collective ability to achieve understanding through modeling. Theory building and empirical study of college and university utility, market, production, and financial functions should be a high-priority research agenda. That also means looking at productivity, because the production function is of key importance. I think there's a lot that can be done on productivity because, after all, Bill Baumol's analogy that a thirty-minute composition for string quartet will always take two man-hours to play applies only to the face-to-face component of teaching. A relatively small proportion of our costs is in that category, and the advent of information technology means that this fraction may even decline. So, there *is* an important research agenda, and I hope that the thinking expressed in this book will help us get on with it.

STEPHEN R. LEWIS, JR.

Carleton College

In Botswana people write praise poems for the chiefs. And I think Larry Lindsey's rewrite of history is an interesting praise poem for Reaganomics. I can't resist, having spent half of my professional life in developing countries, a comment about the four tigers of Asia. Anybody who has looked at it seriously would say that they have *intervened* as much as anybody else but they did it smarter than anybody else. Or, a comment about "capitalist Kenya" which I think is probably better described as a cleptocracy. But to the business at hand.

I'd like to say something about the macroanalysis discussed in the first three chapters. I think we have not examined sufficiently the international implications of what we've been through—the consequences of the expansion of finance from abroad, the trillion-dollar party that we've thrown, and the "hangover" that we're going to have. The uncertainty that I would stress focuses on this: what kind of *international* adjustment mechanism there will be if the United States is going to get things in balance—as I think we must. And, if the other main surplus countries are not going to be expansionary, there's a good possibility that we could end up with both a serious domestic problem and a serious world problem, a development that would put us in very difficult shape.

Dick Eckaus wrote about the quality competition question and used the Howard Bowen observation about "raising all you can and spending all you raise"; others have written about our current cost trajectory. It might be useful to think about these issues in terms of *who* should pay—parents, government, state or local corporations, the foundation world, and so on, and *what* they are paying for. We've paid some attention to the teaching and the research and the public service functions. The other issue that many of us have to deal with is this: what are the quid pro quos in those relationships—with parents and students, with governments, and so on? The consumptionist trend which both Larry Lindsey and Harold Shapiro noted seems to raise some interesting questions. I think Derek Bok's emphasis on prestige rather than other factors on the consumption side is an interesting and useful one. The difficulty with consumerism comes in talking about what it is we are providing, and what people are buying. How do they know what it is, other than what we tell them or what the guidebooks tell them? Who judges the output? Is it the *U.S. News* annual survey, or is it something else? And particularly on the consumerist side, who is to judge the balance between teaching and research or scholarship?

I have also been struck by the emphasis in the essays on the functions of colleges and universities in producing, processing, and transmitting information. We get the stress in Larry Lindsey's chapter on the importance of *liberal arts* education, in teaching people to *think* and to *create* knowledge and information, rather than simply to absorb it. We do both creating and transmitting, and one of the issues is to determine what's the balance, and who's going to pay for the balancing that we do?

On the quality competition that Dick Eckaus stressed, my recollection of what we went through in the 1960s and 1970s is that there was a fairly clear adjustment process. The competition as higher education expanded in the 1960s and the early 1970s, and then as it contracted, was fairly systematic. The adjustment process worked not only within higher education, within the various clusters of institutions that Eckaus mentioned, but also by pulling in resources from outside of higher education. I well remember the North Adams State College in North Adams, Massachusetts, building up a very high-quality faculty by raiding the local high school for extremely effective teachers, and they built an excellent college that way. Then as we got into the glut part of the cycle for Ph.D.s, they went the next step and moved up very substantially in the "credential" quality of their faculty. So, this process of quality competition is *not* simply trading people around within the higher education community but also reaching out—certainly in the sciences, engineering, economics and other areas—beyond academe. And that adjustment process and the quality competition is not something that's a zero-sum game for higher education. We *will* pull resources in from other sectors, and that is the way the process would work.

I also believe we must pay more attention to demographic issues. The most obvious is the decline in the cohort of 18-year-olds before it starts rising again in the mid-1990s. This will, on the basis of historical precedent, raise the economic return to that group in relative terms, which should have some implications for higher education. But I was distressed that the essays did not give more attention to the issue of what happens to racial minorities in the changing demographic mix. One question that all of us, whether public sector or private sector, will be dealing with is a very, very different ethnic mix of high school graduates and incoming students during the next decade—by the end of the next decade for sure. And that is a national problem. We must contribute to creating a work force that is educated fully across ethnic and racial lines in a way that's not the case now. That's something that ought to be high on our agenda, if it is not already.

Another demographic issue not addressed in the essays is what happens on the faculty side, given the projected large number of retirements in the decade of the 1990s. I feel this at Carleton because our tenured faculty tends to be about ten years younger than the national average, and I can see us being raided rather heavily in the next decade since we have a group of people who look very good as department chairs and deans as other faculties retire. The lags in this long cycle on the faculty side are important and are going to affect all of us, whether we are principally buyers or principally sellers of Ph.D.s.

On the question of our cost structure, I think that the Baumol and Bowen "economics of the performing arts" is still critically important for our institutions to understand, particularly those of us who are in the undergraduate business only. For instance, in the more pessimistic secenarios about the macroeconomy—if in fact median family incomes don't go up, and if productivity is not rising and so on—we will not face the same kind of salary pressure *unless* there's something peculiar going on in our demographics. Salary pressure arises when there's productivity growth in the rest of the economy and we've got to bid against it. If things are going well, we're likely not to face the tuition barriers or the public financing barriers. Therefore, we will have the financing to pay those salaries that we need to pay. If things are awful, they're awful for everybody. We may face a lot of tuition resistance and tax resistance, but we also will not have the same kinds of salary pressures, when general productivity growth is slower. We are likely to get into trouble if there are some significant shifts in what's going on in the academic world as compared with other sectors.

On the public/private question, it's *not* obvious that the public institutions come out ahead in the quality competition. In many systems, the 1970s taught us that even though the public *might* have been able to organize things and improve quality, that did not happen to the extent it could have because the politics of those systems are so difficult. Therefore, I think that the private sector may have some advantage in the public/private competition for quality.

On tuition and aid policy—I can't say that I like the way the issues were presented for several reasons. First of all, in all of our institutions tuition covers only part of the cost; to a very large extent the "sticker price" is an arbitrary price. And "aid" is, in effect, a discount from that arbitrary sticker price. Therefore, the definition of what aid *really* constitutes is somewhat ambiguous. To characterize "aid" as a "tax" on the current generation is not appropriate, particularly when the current generation pays, on the full sticker price, only two-thirds or less of the *cost* of the education. The aid issue, and how it is discussed, has been very confusing. It is in *all* of our interests to try to get some clarity and some coherence in how it is understood.

One last comment on the aid side. Having moved from the East to the Midwest, I've been struck by the differences in how one interprets the share of student body on financial aid. It's almost a U-shaped proposition: the very strong institutions tend to have a large share on financial aid because they're trying to diversify their student body, and the very weak institutions have a large share on financial aid because they have to discount heavily in order to fill beds. One can see exactly the same percentage and draw very, very different conclusions from it. That illustrates the issue of how difficult it is to talk sensibly about the aid and tuition nexus of issues.

In closing, let me caution that responses by colleges and universities have to be unique to each institution. All of us have to find ways of dealing with our own particular sets of constituents. Part of this issue is a matter of educating our constituents about the nature of our enterprises, what drives the costs, and how one values the output. This means a continual process of analysis and planning and projecting, not because you can project accurately what's going to happen, but because it's a way of trying to understand better what forces influence our institutions and their economies. We need to get some understanding among parents, taxpayers, trustees, alumni, students, and so on of what constraints we are under and where the pressures come from.

But let's not confuse analysis and understanding with prediction. A trustee of Williams, now deceased, was a man named Van Clark—a wonderful trustee and a wonderfully outrageous fellow. In 1972 he told then-president Jack Sawyer that we were "in fat city" economically. In 1974 after the financial markets had collapsed and the oil price had quadrupled and so on, we were sitting around in the office wondering what had happened. And he said, "Well, we did a lot of planning, but you've got to remember Wright's law of airplane design." I said, "What's that?" And he said, "No airplane has ever crashed off of an *anticipated* failure."

BRUCE JOHNSTONE

State University of New York

As a one-time or would-be economist as well as a representative of the public sector, my comments may reflect both of these attributes, or liabilities, as the case may be.

After reading the chapters—and they are fascinating and certainly provocative—I think the underlying issue is whether the macroeconomy can and will sustain the current cost trajectory of higher education, and if not, how that cost structure will be forced to adapt downward to a substantially different and leaner way of life in the academy.

This issue poses at least three subquestions. First, what are the microeconomic, technological, and political degrees of freedom in our academic production function? That is, to what degree and at what kinds of institutions *can* our current functions of teaching, research, and service be achieved at much lower costs per unit? Second, what changes— assuming that some are at least conceivable—will the currently foreseeable macroeconomic forces pressure us to accept? And finally, should we or can we prepare for these forces and for this downsizing, or should we let the macroeconomic forces, if they are so bent on doing, force upon us these disagreeable changes in the microeconomics of our institutions, with us, our faculties, and our boards dragged along kicking and screaming for the good old days?

Turning to the first question and rephrasing it one more time: *Can* something like higher education be produced in a substantially cheaper way than most of us now produce it? One answer to that, of course, is "yes," because we have "out there" an enormous range of models, with some entities on the fringe of the degree-granting academic world, mostly proprietary, showing that they can produce education quite cheaply. They may look little like the COFHE institutions, and yet they can still be postsecondary and even degree granting, and they fill an evidently needed niche.

In my world of public higher education, there is also an enormous range of cost differentials among the types of institutions even within my own system, more about which I will say in a moment. But what would it require of a COFHE school or of any other mainstream research university to drive its budget down *anywhere near* those proprietary per-student levels? By "mainstream" institution of higher education, I mean one that essentially runs on full-time, tenured or tenure-track faculty, carrying something like two- and three-course loads, with four-course loads in some of the undergraduate colleges, and with an array of student support services. What would it require of us to *substantially* lower our underlying cost structure?

Such a change would inevitably mean faculty with much less of what they most want: lots of time with lots of resources at hand—library resources, fine students (preferably post-doctoral fellows), computer time, travel time, and equipment. Can our faculty function with much less of that time, doing substantially more teaching of more students? And would they still be recognizably "our faculty"? Can we, or how might we, get along with a substantial reduction in the prevailing student support system: far less counseling, far less tutoring, far less advising, far less of the kinds of facilities and amenities that our institutions, by and large, have enhanced ourselves with, presumably in response to student demand? Any of these major changes—and they are wrenching changes—could lower student credit hour unit costs. But how could we get there? And what would be society's loss?

Another way of responding to a macroeconomic pressure for substantially lowered unit costs in higher education could be through lowering the amount of time, and thus the need for resources, toward the degree. This is the old Carnegie Commission recommendation that many of you may recall from the mid-1970s. It was estimated by the commission that going from a four-year to a three-year baccalaureate would save enormous sums through the lower proportion of our gross national product devoted to higher education. Such a change, of course, could do devastating damage to institutions. But such a fundamental change in the time-to-a-degree might be one of the most effective responses to a macroeconomic pressure to substantially reduce the degree cost to the purchasers, be they consumers, students and families, or taxpayers.

Again, the issue, I think, is what the future economy is going to force upon us either through price resistance from consumers in the COFHE institutions, or by taxpayer and legislative resistance in the world of state-supported higher education. It may pose a particular challenge to me. I have 64 campuses in my system, the State University of New York, with 380,000 students, institutions ranging from 30 community colleges, which are locally owned, to state-owned, four-year institutions, to especially interesting campuses like a maritime college, a fashion institute, and the contract land-grant colleges at Cornell, to our four public university centers and two stand-alone health centers, including three teaching hospitals. I have just been invited by the director of the budget in New York State to "try out" a $90-100 million budget cut.

So I'm being challenged to consider this very question: whether there are substantially different—and lower—production functions within these institutions. I am being given a few constraints. That is, the Governor's office negotiates the salary increases, so that degree of freedom is not available to me. We're apparently not supposed to talk about closing institutions, so those degrees of freedom are not there—and, oh yes, we're not supposed to have a tuition increase so . . . It's getting a little hard to see what responses are open to me, but I think what I'm experiencing may be a peek at the macroeconomic challenges discussed in this book by my colleagues. In other words, is this a glimpse at a future in which, for a whole variety of reasons, there will be fundamentally fewer state taxpayer-generated resources available to a public sector like mine? And is that anything like the challenge that might or might not befall the COFHE institutions from a substantial withdrawal of federal resources or a substantial price resistance? I frankly think that the odds are more likely that the public sector rather than the COFHE world will see this fundamental change. I think it is likely that student consumer demand will be more robust, and that federal demand via aid and research grants and indirect overhead may well be more robust than the outright state taxpayer-generated operating grants that are supporting most of the American students in most of the colleges in this country.

So, how should we respond? We could provide less access—but probably should not. Could we shift more burden in the public sector to students and families? In most states, yes. In New York State the tuition issue is heavily politicized at the moment. If we cannot provide less access and simply cut out the enrollments, or if we cannot shift costs to families and students via higher tuitions, then the third alternative opens up: Is there a dramatic change in the way of doing business?

It's tempting to think that the culprit might be the high cost of big research. I think there were suggestions, perhaps in Harold Shapiro's chapter, that there might be some relief either by a greater differentiation of institutional types, or by a lowering of the numbers of institutions or of faculty that have access to that kind of high-cost research. There might be a clearer separation of the undergraduate teaching function from big science research. This separation could help to insulate the undergraduate from the costs of this research.

Translated in terms of my public institution, this could mean that if we concentrate the research even more in the universities at Buffalo and Stony Brook, and even less in the comprehensive colleges, there may be some savings. In reply to that suggestion, however, is Shapiro's observation that there are very substantial demands upon us to *increase* costs associated with undergraduate teaching, particularly in the vulnerable freshman year, with *more* advising, counseling, tutoring and such, so that, contrary to some conventional wisdom, the unit cost of instruction in a predominantly undergraduate college with a minimal research function may not be so different from the cost of instruction in a research university. The college may not have the high costs of equipment, star faculty salaries, or tiny teaching loads—but neither does it have the advantages of mass lectures, inexpensive graduate assistants, and a production function featuring enormous economies of scale. So I'm not sure that a greater differentiation of research from nonresearch institutions is going to help.

My conclusion is that we will continue to see enormous resistance in our academy to fundamental changes in lifestyle and production functions and therefore the unit costs. We may see a slow continuing differentiation of production functions in, for example, the nonselective private institutions or in the public sector. But the COFHE schools are not likely to change their costs greatly.

RICHARD SPIES

Princeton University

My initial reaction to these essays and commentaries is to go right out and tell my investment advisors to unload everything. Anytime economists agree about anything, we're in trouble.

Rather than just repeat what others have already discussed—better than I could—let me limit my remarks to a few comments about the Lindsey paper. In particular, I'd like to concentrate for a few minutes on Larry Lindsey's taxonomy concerning individualism versus statism; and, in particular, how that taxonomy does or does not help us think about the problems and opportunities facing higher education. I do this in part to be helpful and provocative, but I must admit that I also do it to avoid getting myself in too much trouble. I would really like to comment on Dick Eckaus's chapter, but my credentials as a macroeconomist are about 15 years old and never were very good anyway, so I can't really add much to his comments except to say that I agree with most of his arguments. As for Harold Shapiro's comments, Mr. Shapiro is my boss and my mother didn't raise any dummies, so I agree with everything he said.

With respect to Larry Lindsey's paper I will resist the urge to enter the fray and argue about whether our national economic experience of the 1970s is proof of the correctness of what he calls individualism, or alternatively, an indication of how tough it is in our society and with our system of governance, to establish and then implement a reasonable set of government constraints. I am reminded, thinking about that, of a discussion I had earlier in this conference about the difficulty of managing an investment portfolio through an investment committee. Suppose, for example, the investment committee meets on October 16, 1987. It decides that something's about to happen, and it had better do something about it, so it schedules a meeting for the following Friday (which is not too different from what I'm sure happened to many of us during the stock market craziness of that year). Similarly, trying to develop a national economic policy is tough enough, but developing a consensus for that policy is even more difficult.

I also won't mention, in trying to analyze the 1970s, the enormous tax that was imposed on our economy between 1973 and 1980 in the form of higher oil prices, because that would open a whole new Pandora's Box that I don't want to get into. I will also resist the urge to analyze the recovery of the 1980s, and the role of individualism in that recovery, as opposed to the role played by traditional macroeconomic policy. There was, as Dick Eckaus pointed out, clear if unintended Keynesian demand stimulus through tax cuts and increased government spending, plus a very carefully controlled monetary policy, overseen by Paul Volcker and his colleagues, during that period. But I won't say anything about that either.

Having successfully avoided mentioning any of those things, let me instead talk about the relevance of Larry Lindsey's individualism model for higher education. The reason I want to do this is that I think such a model could easily be abused and lead us very far astray, particularly if we allow people like Secretary of Education Bill Bennett to beat us around the head and shoulders with it, which I think has happened in recent years. I am pretty sure that Lindsey—and other "free market" economists—does not intend remarks such as these to be used as an argument for a complete "hands-off" policy toward higher education by the federal government, but unfortunately, they have all too frequently been used in exactly that way. The problem with such an argument is that it can easily be used—or, to be more accurate, abused—to suggest that colleges and universities should be treated like any other private business, with no legitimate government role in the process. Secretary Bennett, for example, might well take Lindsey's arguments a step or two further and conclude that the government should just step back and let Adam Smith's "invisible hand" work its magic in higher education, as it supposedly does in other "business." Thus, my real dispute is not with Lindsey's remarks as they stand—again, I'll be careful *not* to say what I think about that subject—but rather with the potential damage they can cause when extended too simplistically to a whole set of much more complicated national policy issues.

With that as an introduction, basically my message to Larry Lindsey (and to Bill Bennett) would be that Adam Smith, for all of his qualities, would never make it as a university president. And I believe that because I believe colleges and universities are "inherently and unequivocally quasi-, semi-, loosely public and/or private institutions, depending on the circumstances." We really are, as that unequivocal statement suggests, some place in between public and private. And I think that we, society as a whole, and above all, educational policy makers, should recognize that fact.

To some extent this apparent schizophrenia is a matter of our wanting to have our cake and eat it, too. We are very good at going to Washington and pleading for government funds, while at the same time expressing righteous indignation about the narrow-minded, bureaucratic regulation that sometimes accompanies those funds. For *other* kinds of government programs, we would probably argue that such regulation is a reasonable attempt at accountability, but for us it is narrow minded and bureaucratic. But I think, putting aside that tendency to argue out of both sides of our mouths, to a very large extent we really are a mix of private economic actor, in the traditional sense that Adam Smith would have understood that term, and public agent acting on behalf of society as a whole in a manner which is usually reserved for governments. There are lots of examples of our private role which I could go through in great detail, and I'm sure others could add to. Let me give just a few examples: We engage in what is frequently vicious competition among ourselves for students and faculty. We each have a fiercely independent sense of our own very special mission, our own very special role as individual institutions and how we fit into the larger picture. Whatever the beauty contest organizers at *U.S. News & World Report* might say, for example, we at Princeton know that we are doing a better job than Yale and Swarthmore, and even more importantly, that we have chosen a more useful and appropriate definition of the job to do than Yale or Swarthmore. And I'm sure they feel equally strongly about their own roles. And I think that is a large part of what we as a nation gain from the pluralism of higher education in this country.

The public role of colleges and universities is more complicated. And in this case, I believe it is not so much that the products of our industry are somehow or other good for society or that they provide benefits for society as a whole beyond those captured by consumers or producers (i.e., externalities). We believe those products—teaching and research—are, in fact, good for society and do provide external benefits, but I don't think that's the distinguishing characteristic. Indeed, agriculture is useful for the society, but not too many farmers are tax exempt. (They may be on the dole in a different way, but I don't think anyone argues that they belong among the ranks of tax-exempt institutions.) In our case, though, what I think distinguishes us as a public institution is the way we are organized and the way we go about our business, the way in which we set our objectives, and the way in which we go about trying to achieve those objectives. Basically, my conclusion is that Adam Smith's invisible hand doesn't work very well with us, primarily because, indeed solely, because we are not profit maximizers as Adam Smith assumed that the organizations he was studying were.

Adam Smith would not understand a business that practiced price discrimination, not to increase its customer base and thus its revenues (and presumably its profits), but to subsidize individual customers, while at the same time excluding altogether other customers, who don't need or want such a subsidy. Private colleges and universities do that: we call it financial aid or scholarships. And we do it, not in order to increase the number of students, at least most of us don't think of financial aid as a way to increase the number of students, but because we care about the composition of our "customer" base in a way that General Motors does not.

Adam Smith would not understand an institution that takes advantage of technology—computers have been mentioned several times—but takes advantage of that technology not to reduce labor costs, but to make the final product more complicated, and thus more expensive rather than less expensive. But that's exactly what we do with computers and with most forms of technology.

Adam Smith would not understand a business that subsidizes one product line, not as a loss leader, but because our employees and some of our other customers think that that line of work would be fun. We do that in the form of cost-sharing on sponsored research—which really is, at least in most of our institutions, driven by the intellectual curiosity of individual faculty, and to a lesser extent students, rather than by some overall institutional business plan. (Not only that, in addition to subsidizing the work itself, we almost give away the outcome of that work by publishing our results.)

Adam Smith would not understand a business that insists on sustaining its allegiance to one product line—the liberal arts—even though many of its customers want a more relevant, more vocation-oriented offering; or an institution that is more nervous about a budget surplus than a budget deficit, which most of us are; that takes pride in charging students, its customers, only 60 percent of the cost of the service it is providing them, relying on a sophisticated tithing process to make up the rest of the cost; that mixes its employees together with its customers and lets both of them tell the president what to do, and then tells the president that he or she has to listen to what they say.

Adam Smith or Larry Lindsey (or Bill Bennett), no matter what you think about the appropriate way to manage economic activity in the country as a whole, I'd say, please, don't make the mistake of thinking about colleges and universities as just another form of private business. The world is really too complicated for that. We are, as I said earlier, "inherently and unequivocally quasi-, semi-, loosely public and/or private, depending on the circumstances." And we insist on being treated that way—as long as it works to our advantage, at least. To be slightly more serious, but only slightly, I think we insist on being treated that way, as long as it works to the advantage of our students and the other publics we serve. And I at least would argue that it does.

One final, unrelated thought about the current situation and whether we should be pessimistic or optimistic about the present and the future. I think, as Bill Massy mentioned earlier, it is useful to dig up the snakes occasionally. But it's also useful to remember that people have been doing that for a long time, and so far at least, we're still a few steps ahead of them. I was reminded of that when Princeton announced that it had an operating budget deficit for 1987–88. A faculty friend, after reading the official announcement of that deficit, sent me a copy of a *Princeton Alumni Weekly* article from sometime back in the 1950s—I don't remember the exact date—in which the university reported a similar deficit. The article described that problem as the result of an overrun in the purchase of library books and a shortfall in the alumni fund, which is exactly what we experienced in 1987—88. It gave me some consolation to know we weren't the first to experience such problems. At the same time, even though some things don't change, lots of things have changed at Princeton and at most of our institutions. I believe that Princeton is a measurably and significantly better institution than it was 30 years ago, when this earlier deficit took place. This is because significant new resources have been attracted since then, and I think these resources have been invested in a way that has made Princeton a better place. I'm not saying that every investment has been just right, but on average, I think these resources have been used wisely. That doesn't mean that we're not constantly trying to expand our reach, that our vision isn't outdistancing our reach at all times: But it does mean that we should not be too pessimistic about either the present or the future. We clearly must work hard at trying to make ourselves better, but we should not ignore the value and importance of what has already been accomplished. And part of that, I think, is to continue to adhere to the kind of private/public mix that most of us have attained and have managed successfully for some time, and to continue to make our case to the various publics we are serving.

BIBLIOGRAPHY

ANDERSON, RICHARD E., and WILLIAM F. MASSY. "The Economic Outlook and What it Means for Colleges and Universities." *Capital Ideas* 4, no. 3 (October 1989).

ANDERSON, RICHARD E., and JOEL W. MEYERSON, EDS. *Financial Planning Under Economic Uncertainty*, San Francisco: Jossey-Bass, 1990.

ANDERSON, RICHARD E., and JOEL W. MEYERSON, EDS. *Financing Higher Education in a Global Economy*, New York: ACE/Macmillan, 1990.

ANDERSON, RICHARD E., and JOEL W. MEYERSON, EDS. *Financing Higher Education: Strategies After Tax Reform.* San Francisco: Jossey-Bass, 1987.

Association of American Universities. *Financing and Managing University Research Equipment*, Washington, DC: Association of American Universities, 1985.

ASSOCIATION OF AMERICAN UNIVERSITIES. *The Scientific Instrumentation Needs of Research Universities.* Washington, DC: A Report to the National Science Foundation, 1980.

ASSOCIATION OF GOVERNING BOARDS. *Financial Responsibilities of Governing Boards.* Washington, DC: Association of Governing Boards, 1985.

BERGSTEN, C. FRED. *America in the World Economy: A Strategy for the 1990's.* Washington, DC: Institute for International Economics, 1988.

BERGSTEN, C. FRED, and WILLIAM R. CLINE. *The United States-Japan Economic Problem.* Washington, DC: Institute for International Economics, 1985.

BOWEN, HOWARD R. *The Costs of Higher Education.* San Francisco: Jossey-Bass, 1980.

BOWEN, WILLIAM G. *The Economics of the Major Private Universities.* Berkeley, CA: Carnegie Commission on the Future of Higher Education, 1968.

BRYANT, RALPH C., GERALD HOLTHAM, and PETER HOOPER, EDS. *External Deficits and the Dollar: The Pit and the Pendulum.* Washington, DC: The Brookings Institution, 1988.

FRIEDMAN, BENJAMIN M. *Day of Reckoning: The Consequences of American*

Economic Policy Under Reagan and After. New York: Random House, 1988.

LITAN, ROBERT E., ROBERT Z. LAWRENCE, and CHARLES L. SCULTZE, EDS. *American Living Standards: Threats and Challenges*. Washington, DC: The Brookings Institution, 1988.

MALABRE, ALFRED L., JR. *Beyond Our Means*. New York: Random House, 1987.

MARRIS, STEPHAN. *Deficits and the Dollar: The World Economy at Risk*. Washington, DC: Institute for International Economics, 1985.

PETERSON, PETER G., and NEIL HOWE. *On Borrowed Time: How the Growth in Entitlement Spending Threatens America's Future*. New York: Simon & Schuster, 1989.

Appendix

KEY ECONOMIC INDICATORS FOR HIGHER EDUCATION

CAROL FRANCES

The 1990s will be a forward-looking decade, with attention drawn ahead to the twenty-first century. Preparations for the future may be misguided, however, if they are based on projections that turn out to be wrong—and projections are often wrong, usually for unexpected reasons. A more effective approach to preparing for the future is to be alert to ongoing change, and resilient in responding to new challenges and opportunities.

Some articulate leaders in higher education argue that the most important job for management of the nation's colleges and universities in the coming decade is slimming down to operate more successfully in hard times. Others, scanning the horizon of political upheaval and economic change across both hemispheres, conclude that the most important task of leadership in higher education is taking up the challenges and opportunities of playing a greater role in a resurgent America.

Both are right. And both can fuel their engines with better economic information.

Key economic indicators may be helpful in recognizing changes that affect higher education and in getting an early start in anticipating what these changes might mean for different sectors and individual institutions.

This appendix is a report of a continuing project to develop economic indicators for higher education. The project was originally spon-

Carol Frances is the president of Carol Frances + Associates, a firm that specializes in the economics and finance of higher education.

sored by Coopers & Lybrand and is now moving forward in cooperation with the National Association of College and University Business Officers. The purpose of the project is to identify key indicators of the major economic trends impacting on higher education; to provide the latest available trend data for each indicator; to identify changes in these trends; and, most important, to begin the search for the potential implications for higher education.

Some of the indicators based on national trend data have regional, state, or local analogs that could be collected by colleges and universities doing their own environmental scanning and education market analysis.

Information for most of these economic indicators can be collected from secondary sources, particularly annual editions of the Economic Report of the President prepared by the Council of Economic Advisors, and the Statistical Abstract published by the U.S. Department of Commerce. More up-to-date primary sources for the data are listed following this appendix.

KEY ECONOMIC INDICATORS FOR HIGHER EDUCATION
POTENTIAL DEMAND FOR HIGHER EDUCATION

1. Gross national product

2. Population
   2.1 Population by age group
   2.2 High school graduates
   2.3 College-going rates

3. Labor force
   3.1 Employment/unemployment
   3.2 New entrants

REVENUES

4. State budgets
   4.1 State appropriations for higher education
   4.2 Real state appropriations for higher education per student
   4.3 State budget surplus/deficit as a percent of state budget expenditures

5. Federal budget
   5.1 Federal budget deficit/surplus
   5.2 Federal appropriations for student financial aid
   5.3 Federal research grants and contracts

POTENTIAL DEMAND FOR HIGHER EDUCATION

1. GROSS NATIONAL PRODUCT
HIGHER EDUCATION AS SECTOR OF THE U.S. ECONOMY

Higher education, in 1990, is an economic enterprise of close to $150 billion in revenues, produced by more than 3,500 colleges and universities including their branch campuses, employing more than 2.5 million people, and serving more than 13 million students.

Higher education employment is about twice as large as the aerospace industry, and three times bigger than the automobile manufacturing industry.

Expenditures for higher education have held between 2.5 and 2.7 percent of gross national product from 1970 through the 1980s.

IMPACT OF THE ECONOMY ON HIGHER EDUCATION

To analyze the impact of the economy on higher education it is essential at the outset to separate the different effects of longer-term, fundamental trends; shorter-term business cycles; and one-time events in the economy, particularly as they impact on college enrollments.

Chart A1-1 shows the trends in college enrollment over the last 50 years together with an economic chronology intended to be helpful in identifying the possible effects of trends, cycles, and one-time events.

Over the long term, economic growth and prosperity has resulted in growth of higher education as demand for more education increases and people are willing to spend more of an increasing amount of discretionary income to invest in greater learning.

While the longer-term relationship between economic growth and higher education is positive, over the shorter-term business cycle the relationship between higher education and the economy can be negative—that is, higher education is generally countercyclical. The clearest manifestation of this is the increase in enrollment that typically occurs during recessions when people out of work go back to college to prepare themselves for a better position when the economy picks up again and they go back to work.

Recessions are indicated on Chart A1.1 by the black bars. As can be seen on the chart, college enrollment has increased in almost all of the eight recessions since 1945.

One-time economic/political events also have an impact on college enrollment. Expansion of eligibility for student financial aid in 1972 was reflected in the growth of enrollment in the 1970s, and the restriction of eligibility for middle income students in the 1981 budget reconciliation act was a factor in the sideways movement of enrollment in the early 1980s.

Misreading the one-time signals has been a serious problem for higher education—as when, for instance, the run-up in enrollment in 1975 and the drop in 1976 were interpreted as the start of a long-term period of slow growth and even decline in college enrollment when, in fact, it recorded the response to the end of eligibility for education benefits of veterans of the Korean War.

Comparatively speaking, too little attention has been focused on

CHART A1.1. CHRONOLOGY OF ECONOMIC CYCLES AND POLITICAL
EVENTS THAT HAVE AFFECTED COLLEGE ENROLLMENTS

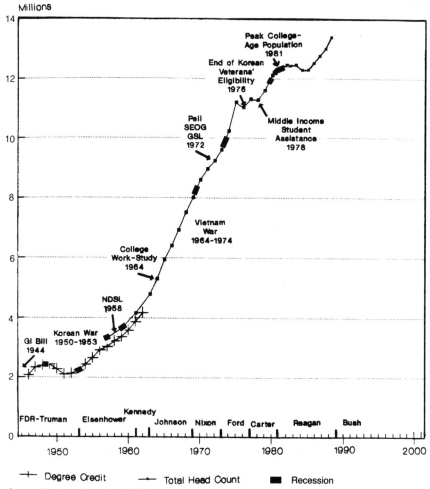

Source: Based on data from NCES.

the impact of economic trends on higher education and too much attention has been focused on the demographic trends. Chart A1.2 shows an
index of the trends in college enrollment compared with indexes of
trends in gross national product and in the size of the traditional college-
age population. The chart indicates that college enrollment over the last
20 years has tracked growth in the overall economy much closer than it
has tracked trends in the college-age population.

When the preliminary estimates of college enrollment for academic
year 1988–89 came in at 13.5 million, even the officials in the National

CHART A1.2. COMPARATIVE TRENDS: COLLEGE ENROLLMENT/GNP/18–24 (Index: 1970 = 100)

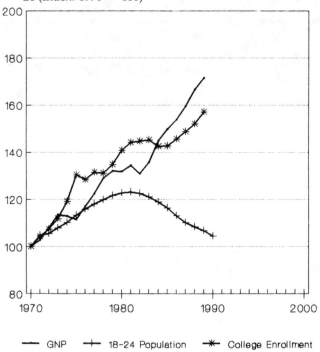

Source: USDE, USDC.

Center for Education Statistics were hesitant to believe it could be up so high. The enrollment total represented an actual increase over the 12.1 million level for 1980–81 of more than 10 percent. Remember that many analysts had projected declines in college enrollment as steep as 15 percent.

2. POPULATION

Demographic trends are extremely important to higher education but planners got into trouble in the 1970s and 1980s paying too much attention to demographic trends and too little attention to economic trends. Demographics drives elementary and secondary enrollments because at the earlier ages, virtually all of the members of the age group are enrolled in school.

The size of the traditional college-age population is useful for pre-

CHART A2.1. COMPARATIVE TRENDS: COLLEGE ENROLLMENT/GNP/18–24 (Index: 1970 = 100)

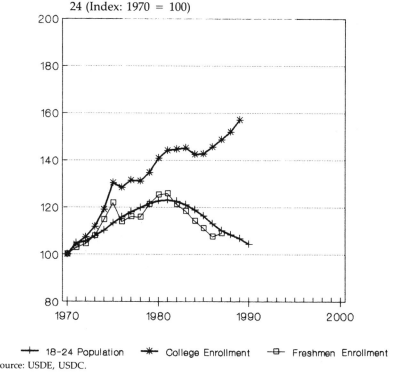

—+— 18-24 Population   —*— College Enrollment   —□— Freshmen Enrollment

Source: USDE, USDC.

dicting trends in freshmen enrollment, but not in total college enrollments, as shown on Chart A2.1. At the present time, less than half of college enrollment is within the traditional "college-age" group 18 to 24 years old.

A more balanced approach combining both demographic and economic information is needed in the 1990s. And in doing demographic analysis to support education policy development and institutional planning for most colleges and universities, it is useful to examine trends for all the major age groups, as shown on Chart A2.2.

Looking at the trends in the size of all the major age groups reveals important differences in the comparative trends in the 1970s, 1980s, and 1990s. In the 1970s, all the age groups from which college enrollments are drawn increased, while the numbers of youngsters age 5 to 17 decreased year-by-year. In the 1980s, the traditional college-age population group declined significantly, but those declines were partially offset by continuing increases in the age groups 25 and over. Meanwhile, the younger age group 5 to 17 moved sideways in a flat-bottomed valley. In

CHART A2.2. TRENDS IN THE POPULATION, BY AGE, 1970–2000

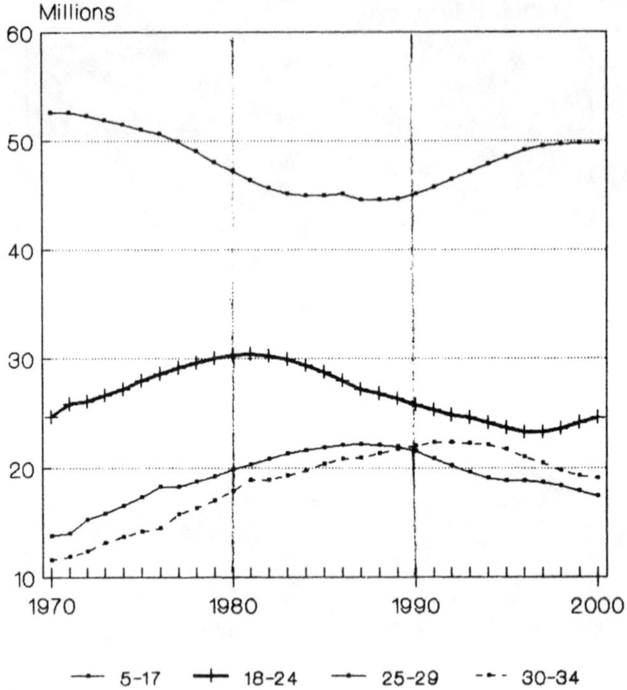
Millions
60
50
40
30
20
10
1970
1980
1990
2000
5-17
18-24
25-29
30-34

Source: Bureau of the Census.

sharp contrast, in the 1990s, the college-age population will continue to decline through 1996, though at a slower pace, but there is no offsetting upsurge in the age groups 25 to 34 because in this decade they also turn down. And, in the 1990s, the younger age group needing elementary and secondary education increases sharply.

Thus, in the 1970s, the college-age population (more properly defined as age 18 and over) grew while the elementary and secondary population (age 5 to 17) declined. In the 1990s, the opposite will be true—college-age populations will decline while elementary and secondary populations will increase. These diverging demographic trends can be expected to pressure federal and state budgets. In the political arena, it will take skill to avoid being pitted against each other in budget negotiations.

In the past, enrollment projections have been made using models driven primarily by demographics as shown below. In the future, enrollment projections should be made using models incorporating more economic, social, and political information that is reflected in college-going rates, as shown in Chart A2.3.

CHART A2.3. ENROLLMENT PROJECTIONS

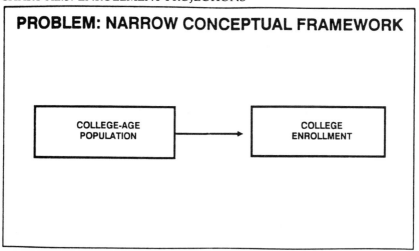

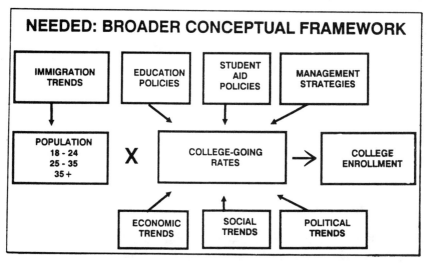

For example, the gap in college-going rates for 18- and 19-year-olds widened in the 1980s between those of whites and those of blacks and Hispanics, as shown on Chart A2.4. Increasing college-going rates of white youth have offset the decline in the size of the population group to produce increases in enrollment. There have not been increases in the college-going rates of blacks to offset college-age population declines, hence black college enrollment declined in the first half of the 1980s. Turnaround in minority enrollment in the 1990s will require significant attention to the college-going rates of minorities.

CHART A2.4. COLLEGE-GOING RATES, 18–19-YEAR-OLDS, BY RACE

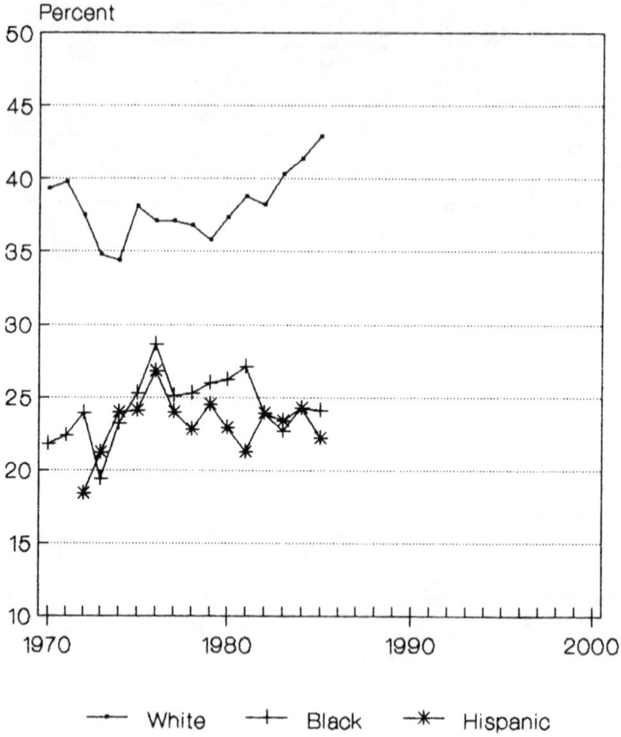

Source: Calculated from Census data.

3. LABOR FORCE

From 1988 to 2000, the United States will need to educate and train over 40 million new entrants to the labor force. The skills required to function in the high-tech and service jobs are advancing, and many of the new entrants—most of whom will be women, minorities, and immigrants—are underprepared for the workplace.

In the 1990s, the labor force will grow at the slowest rate in the 20th century, as shown on Chart A3.1. The slow growth of the labor force is the result of the progression into the next decade of the same demographic trend that resulted in the decline in the 18- to 24-year-old college-age group in the 1980s. While the net increase in the labor force is comparatively small, the net increase of 19 million is the result of 42 million new entrants and 22 million leavers. The national education and training needs relate to the 42 million total new entrants, not to the 19

CHART A3.1. U.S. LABOR FORCE TRENDS IN THE 20th CENTURY

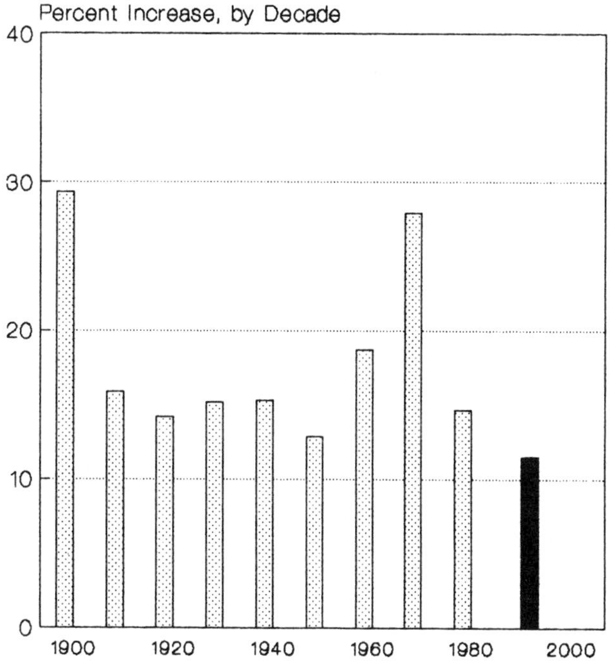

Percent Increase, by Decade

Source: U.S. Department of Labor.

million net new entrants. The changes in the U.S. labor force are shown on Charts A3.2 and A3.3. Thus, the education and training needs are huge and will contribute to sustained demand for higher education in the 1990s.

In addition to the new entrants, large numbers of workers, facing dislocation when their jobs are changed or moved elsewhere, will need education and training. Surveys done for the U.S. Department of Labor indicate that over recent five-year periods, close to one out of every twelve workers, or 10 million total, are displaced. Some of the needed education and training will be provided by industry, and some may be provided by the two-year and four-year colleges.

Trends in the labor force, employment, and unemployment impact higher education and indicators showing their movements are useful in understanding both college enrollments and financial pressures on the institutions.

The total number of people employed in higher education reaches close to 2.5 million in 1990, as shown in Chart A3.4. Trends in employment in higher education correspond to trends in total employment in the nation. In a recession, employment in higher education declines—

CHART A3.2. GROWTH OF THE U.S. LABOR FORCE: 1988–2000

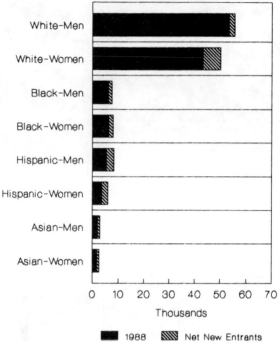

Source: U.S. Department of Labor.

CHART A3.3. CHANGES IN THE U.S. LABOR FORCE BY RACE AND GENDER, 1988–2000

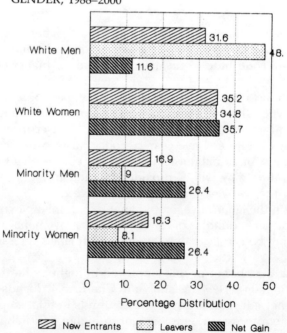

Source: USDL Employment Projections.

CHART A3.4. EMPLOYMENT IN HIGHER EDUCATION (Annual Averages)

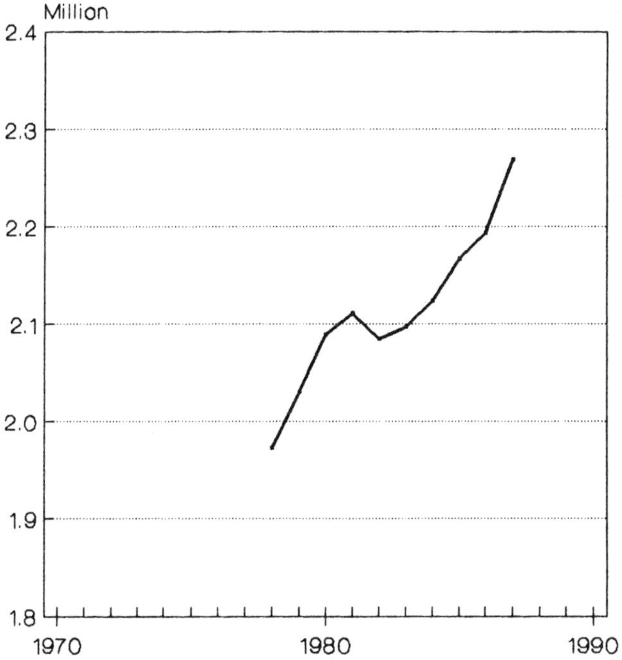

Million

Source: U.S. Department of Labor.

but college enrollment is countercyclical and in a recession it generally increases. The decrease in employment and the increase in enrollment in the last national economic slowdown, in 1981–82, are shown in the indexes in Chart A3.5. This is a typical pattern and explains why colleges and universities experience operational and financial pressures during recessions.

REVENUES

Total revenues for higher education have grown from $66 billion in FY 1980, to $100 billion in 1985, and are projected to exceed $150 billion in 1990.

Revenues are generated from both public and private sources. The public sources include state appropriations primarily for instruction, and federal grants and contracts primarily for student financial aid and research. The private sources include tuition paid by students and their families, annual gifts from individuals, foundations and corporations, endowment income, and revenues from auxiliary enterprises including bookstores and dormitories.

CHART A3.5. COMPARATIVE GROWTH IN COLLEGE ENROLLMENT AND EMPLOYMENT (Index: 1978 = 100)

—•— Employment   —+— Enrollment

Source: USDE, USDL.

Both public and private colleges and universities obtain revenues from both public and private sources, but the profile of sources differs significantly by sector. However, over the 1980s in both sectors, a significant share of the increased revenues has come from private sources.

Chart A4.1 shows trends in the sources of college and university revenues from 1979–80 to 1985–86.

4. STATE BUDGETS

State appropriations for higher education are a significant source of revenue for the public colleges and universities, and in some states to private institutions, as well. State appropriations for higher education have increased significantly in recent years; however, after adjusting for enrollment increases and inflation, the real dollars per student has just exceeded levels reached in the late 1970s, as shown on Chart A4.2.

CHART A4.1. INCREASES IN CURRENT FUND REVENUES BY SOURCE, 1979–1980 to 1985–1986

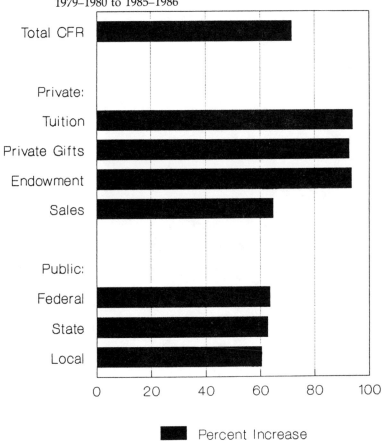

Source: U.S. Department of Education.

In contrast with the federal government, the states have been generating surpluses in recent years. The surpluses are largely in social insurance and pension trust funds, however, as shown on Chart A4.3, and are not available for current program operations.

The states have experienced intensified budget pressures as the federal government shifted responsibility for domestic social programs to the states. As a consequence, increases in support for higher education did not keep pace with college costs, and an increasing share of the cost was shifted to the students. This shift in the student share was a significant factor in explaining the steep increases in tuition in the early 1980s. These trends are shown in Chart A4.4.

CHART A4.2. STATE HIGHER EDUCATION APPROPRIATIONS PER STUDENT, 1973–1986

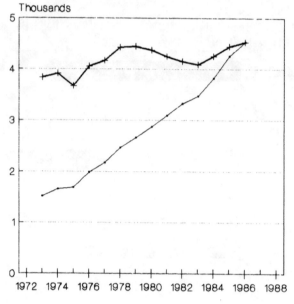

Sources: Calculated using SHEEO, NCES, and HEPI data.

CHART A4.3. TRENDS IN STATE BUDGET SURPLUS/DEFICIT AS A PERCENT OF TOTAL EXPENDITURES

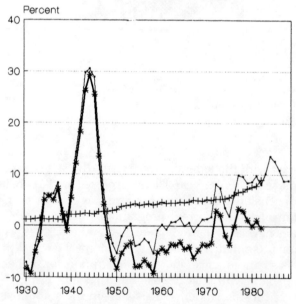

Source: USDC, National Income Accounts.

CHART A4.4. RELATIONSHIP BETWEEN INCREASES IN STATE COLLEGE TUITION AND STATE COLLEGE APPROPRIATIONS

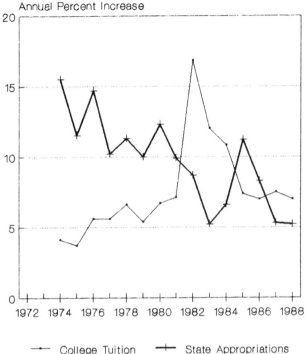

Annual Percent Increase

—•— College Tuition   —+— State Appropriations

Source: State Higher Education Executive Officers.

5. FEDERAL BUDGET
5.1. FEDERAL BUDGET DEFICIT

The federal budget deficit loomed over education budget negotiations throughout the 1980s and it persists into the 1990s. Though the United States has not had a balanced federal budget since 1969, the deficit increased dramatically in the 1980s as shown on Chart A5.1. Federal expenditures stayed at about the same share of the gross national product throughout the 1980s, but federal revenues decreased significantly as a share of GNP as a result of the 1981 reduction in federal income taxes. The deficit grew because of revenue shortfalls, not increased spending.

5.2. ALLOCATION OF FEDERAL REVENUES TO EDUCATION AND TRAINING

Though federal budget revenues declined as a share of GNP, federal revenues did, in fact, increase from 1980 to 1988 by $474 billion. Of the

CHART A5.1. U.S. BUDGET SURPLUS/DEFICIT

Source: Congressional Budget Office.

increase, $156 billion was spent for defense, $100 billion for interest, and less than $1 billion was spent for education and training. The allocation of the increase in federal budget revenues by major function is shown on Chart A5.2. The comparative trends in federal outlays for defense and for education and training over the period from 1940 to 1990 is shown on Chart A5.3.

5.3. FEDERAL EXPENDITURES FOR RESEARCH AND DEVELOPMENT

Federal funding is the major source of support for research and development performed by the colleges and universities. Research and development escaped much of the federal budget cutting and increased from 1980 to 1988.

While the amount of federal funding increased, the amount supported by the colleges and universities increased even more. The share of the research performed by colleges and universities that is self-

CHART A5.2. FEDERAL BUDGET ALLOCATIONS FOR NATIONAL PRIORITIES

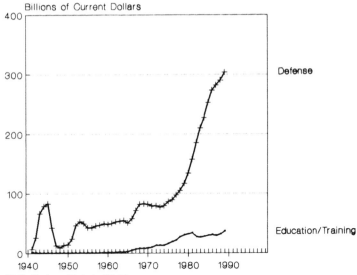

Source: OMB, Budget, Historical Tables.

CHART A5.3. INCREASE IN FEDERAL BUDGET OUTLAYS, BY FUNCTION, 1980–1988

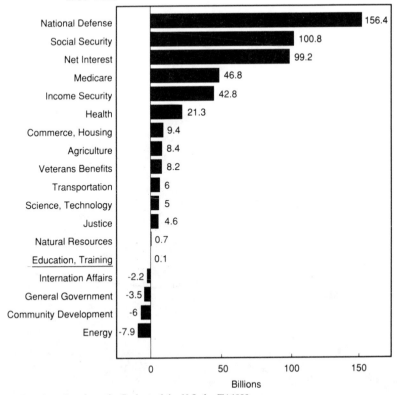

Source: Based on data from the Budget of the U.S. for FY 1990.

funded has doubled from about 8 percent to over 16 percent, as shown on Chart A5.4.

While the number of federal dollars for research performed by universities per dollar of their own funds has declined substantially since it peaked in the early 1960s, the relatively small number of state dollars per dollar of university self-funding of R&D has also declined. The dollars of industry funding per university dollar, though it has been inching up in recent years, remains very low and still below the levels in the late 1950s. The trends in federal, state, and industry funding of university R&D per dollar of their own funds is shown on Chart A5.5.

Greater self-funding by universities of their own research is adding to the financial pressures experienced by these institutions.

6. VOLUNTARY SUPPORT FOR HIGHER EDUCATION

With public support from both federal and state governments growing at a slower pace than base level expenditures, the colleges and universities have relied on private sources of support to a greater extent.

CHART A5.4. PERCENT OF UNIVERSITY R&D THAT IS SELF-FUNDED

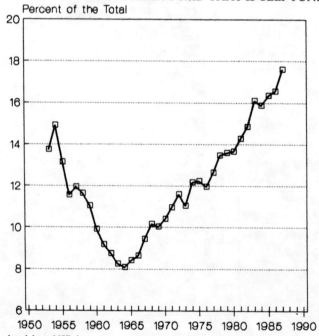

Source: Calculated from NSF data.

CHART A5.5. DOLLARS OF OUTSIDE R&D FUNDING PER DOLLAR OF
UNIVERSITY R&D SELF-FUNDING

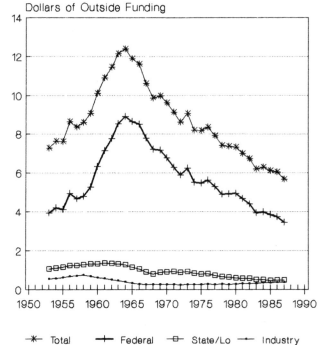

Dollars of Outside Funding

—*— Total   —+— Federal   —⊟— State/Lo   —•— Industry

Source: Calculated from NSF data.

Total voluntary support for higher education increased to over $8.5 billion in 1988, as shown on Chart A6.1.

Pressures on the colleges and universities to find revenues to balance current operating budgets have resulted in a larger share of the voluntary support being spent for current operations and a smaller share used for capital investment or building endowment, as shown on Chart A6.2. The share of voluntary support invested for the benefit of future students is an economic indicator that provides good insights into the financial conditions and prospects of the colleges and universities.

7. CORPORATE PROFITS

Corporate profits are initial sources of much of the private support for higher education, either directly as sources for giving from the corporations or through their foundations, or as the source of wealth reflected

CHART A6.1. TRENDS IN VOLUNTARY SUPPORT OF HIGHER EDUCATION

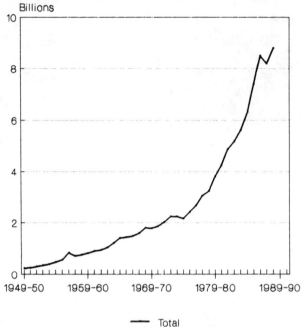

Source: Council for Aid to Education.

CHART A6.2. TRENDS IN SHARE OF VOLUNTARY SUPPORT ALLOCATED TO CAPITAL PURPOSES

Source: Council for Aid to Education.

in the appreciated assets that constitute most of the large donations of individuals to colleges and universities. Corporate profits are a useful economic indicator to track trends in possible sources of private support for higher education.

Long-term, structural shifts in corporate profits should be watched for their implications for higher education. Corporate profits may be paid out as dividends, or retained as undistributed profits. Beginning in the late 1970s, there was a sharp drop in the share of undistributed profits, as shown on Chart A7.1. The reduction of the share of earnings retained may have been a response to fears of management about attracting unwanted offers for mergers and acquisitions.

The question for higher education is whether the net effect on private giving to the colleges and universities from increased dividends received by individuals, and reduced retained earnings held by corporations, is positive or negative—after sorting out the effect on private giving that resulted from reduction in the tax rates in the 1981 Economic Recovery and Tax Act.

CHART A7.1. TRENDS IN CORPORATE PROFITS (Billions of Current Dollars)

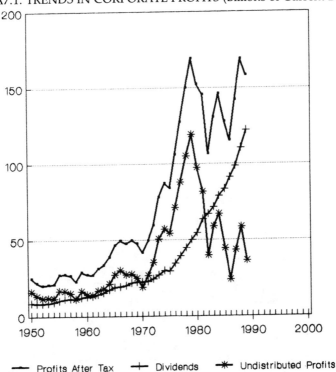

Source: Bureau of Economic Analsis.

8. ENDOWMENT EARNINGS

The share of the returns on endowment transferred as income to current operating budgets constitutes a small but vital source of funds for the colleges and universities. Income from endowment is about 6 percent of the current operating revenues for the private colleges and less than 2 percent for the public colleges. These funds are, however, important resources for quality improvement and program innovation.

Endowments grow as the net result of additions from private giving, increases from returns on invested funds, and decreases resulting from spending of yield and appreciation transferred to the current operating budgets. Some institutions track their experience against a performance objective of reinvesting or spending endowment returns to maintain a fixed real contribution from endowment income to educational costs per student, or an increasing contribution reflecting longer-term quality improvement objectives.

Endowment growth may be a useful economic indicator for colleges and universities with endowments, or those planning to build endowments, in spite of the difficulties in making comparisons among institutions because of differences in valuation and reporting practices.

While endowments have grown spectacularly in market value in the 1980s, as shown on Chart A8.1, real dollars per student had only

CHART A8.1. COLLEGE AND UNIVERSITY ENDOWMENT TRENDS, 1970–1971 to 1985–1986

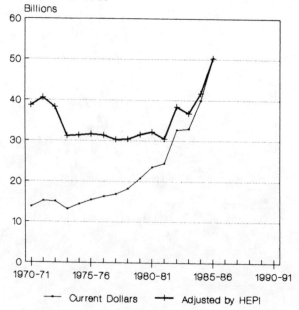

recovered from the losses after the stock market crash in 1973 by the mid-1980s, as shown on Chart A8.2.

EXPENDITURE/COSTS

Costs and cost containment are of keen interest to the colleges and universities, and to the consituents who provide the funding.

Trends in higher education costs by major component are shown on Chart A9.1. For every category, the increase from 1982 (the year of peak rates of increase) to 1989, was less than the rate for the previous seven years (from 1975 to 1982).

9. HIGHER EDUCATION PRICE INDEX

The best available measure of inflation in higher education is the Higher Education Price Index (HEPI)—constructed and maintained by Kent Halstead of Research Associates in Washington.

The annual rates of increase in HEPI since the early 1960s are shown

CHART A8.2. REAL DOLLARS PER STUDENT, 1970–1971 to 1985–1986

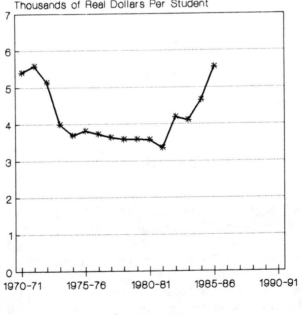

CHART A9.1. TRENDS IN HIGHER EDUCATION COSTS BY COMPONENT

HEPI	74.7 / 42.7
Faculty Salaries	55.4 / 48.3
Staff Wages	73.3 / 32.8
Fringe Benefits	119.1 / 68.5
Services	66.7 / 36.4
Supplies	73.1 / 16.4
Equipment	65.4 / 20.1
Books / Periodicals	102.1 / 52.6
Utilities	190.6 / -7.8

Percent Increase

■ 1975–1982   ▨ 1982–1989

Source: Research Associates.

in Chart A9.2. The run-up in inflation in the late 1970s and early 1980s significantly eroded the economic base of higher education. The slow-down in inflation in the middle and late 1980s was very beneficial as it enabled the colleges and universities to restore some or most of the losses in their financial, physical, and human asset bases.

10. CONSUMER PRICE INDEX

Inflation in the prices consumers pay is measured by the Consumer Price Index (CPI). Higher education has been challenged by government officials, and by the media, to explain why higher education costs and tuition increased faster in the early 1980s than the CPI and why it has slowed less than the CPI since then. Trends in the CPI and in tuition are shown on Chart A10.1.

Tuition is not a "price" like other prices in the CPI because it is driven not only by the underlying costs—as are prices of the goods and

CHART A9.2. HIGHER EDUCATION PRICE INDEX

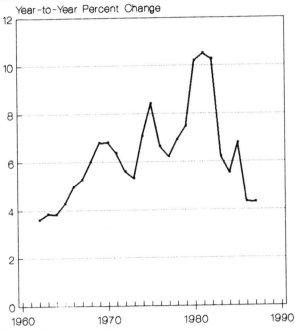

Year-to-Year Percent Change

Source: Kent Halstead, Research Associates.

CHART A10.1. TRENDS IN COLLEGE TUITION COMPARED WITH THE CPI

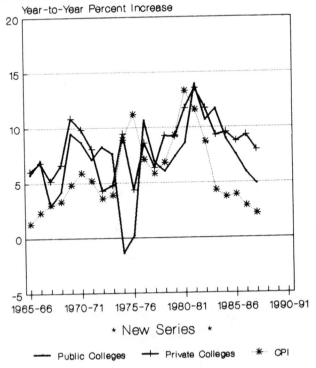

Year-to-Year Percent Increase

* New Series *

—— Public Colleges —+— Private Colleges * CPI

Source: USDE, USDC.

services in the consumer's market basket—but also by the *share* of the costs borne by students. Tuition increases were higher than the increase in the CPI in the 1980s, not primarily because the underlying costs in higher education were increasing at a faster rate than in the 1970s, but because a larger *share* of the costs was being shifted to the students.

11. TRENDS IN FACULTY SALARIES

Faculty and staff salaries generally constitute from two-thirds to three-quarters of the current operating budgets of colleges and universities. Trends in faculty and staff salaries—whether determined by supply and demand in national or local markets or negotiated with collective bargaining agents—are evaluated by the recipients in relation to trends in the cost of living. Thus, trends in the real income of faculty, adjusted for inflation, are useful economic indicators for understanding current

CHART A11.1. FACULTY SALARIES—CPI: Difference in Annual Rates of Change—Annual Real Income Gains/Losses

CF + A calculated from BLS and AAUP data.

costs of higher education. They are also useful in projecting future costs if faculty salaries are above or below longer-term trends in real income.

Annual differences in the rate of increase in faculty salaries and in the CPI are shown on Chart A11.1. While the faculty gained real income in the 1960s, they lost real income in the 1970s, which was not entirely recovered in the 1980s. Thus, faculty enter the 1990s with real incomes at about the levels achieved in the late 1970s, as shown on Chart A11.2, with the annual differences cumulated over time.

ABILITY TO PAY FOR COLLEGE

Trends in the ability to pay—or willingness to borrow—for college are important in understanding actual demand for college education. Economic indicators reflecting trends in student and family resources to pay for college include family income, disposable income per capita, sav-

CHART A11.2. TRENDS IN THE REAL INCOME OF FACULTY: Cumulative Gains/Losses From Base Years 1961 and 1971

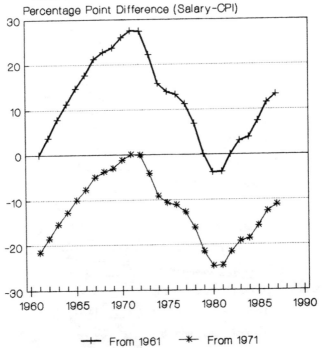

Percentage Point Difference (Salary–CPI)

From 1961   From 1971

CF + A calculated from BLS and AAUP data.

CHART A12.1. TRENDS IN THE ABILITY TO PAY FOR COLLEGE:
COMPARISON OF RATES OF INCREASE IN TUITION AND
INCOME, 1980–1985

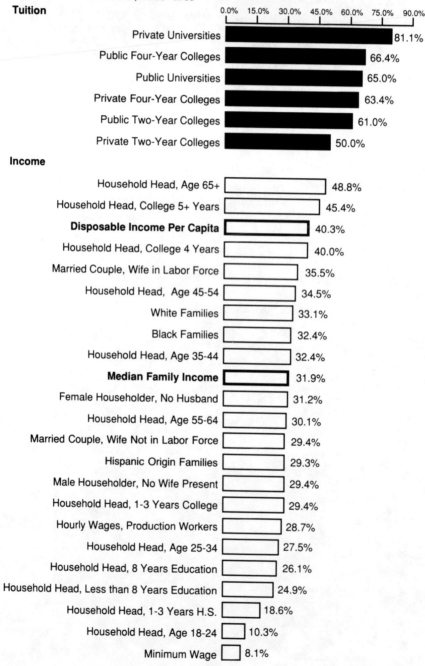

ings, and other borrowing. The availability of student financial aid is also critical.

12. INCOME

Tuition increases in the first half of the 1980s exceeded the increases in the resources students and their families had to pay for college. There are debates over what measure is the best measure of resources to pay for college, so Chart A12.1. shows the increases in several different types of income to many different types of households, from 1980 to 1985, as compared with the increases in tuition for public and private colleges and universities.

12.1 MEDIAN FAMILY INCOME, BY RACE

Trends in median family income by race in constant 1987 dollars are shown on Chart A12.2. On average, white, black, and Hispanic families

CHART A12.2. MEDIAN HOUSEHOLD INCOME, BY RACE

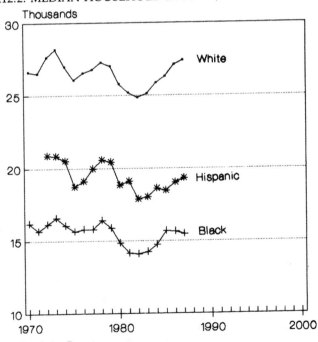

Source: Current Population Reports.

CHART A12.3. PERCENT OF WHITE INCOME

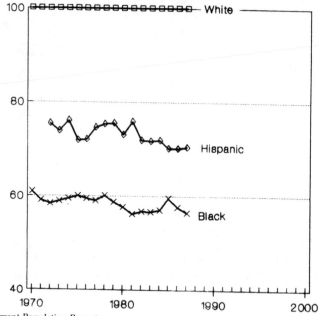

Source: Current Population Reports.

all experienced an erosion of their real income due to high inflation in the late 1970s and early 1980s. But white families have recovered more completely than have the black and Hispanic families.

The same income trend data with minority median family income calculated as a percentage of the white level is shown on Chart A12.3. This shows the declining relative economic position of minority families over the 1980s which created greater financial barriers for them in paying for college, and greater need for financial aid.

13. SAVINGS

Savings is one economic indicator of resources to pay for college. The long-term decline since the early 1970s in savings as a percentage of disposable personal income and the reversal of the trend since the mid-1980s is shown on Chart A13.1.

CHART A13.1. PERSONAL SAVINGS AS A PERCENT OF DISPOSABLE
PERSONAL INCOME

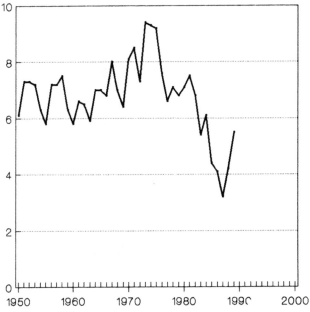

Source: Economic Report, 1990.

14. CONSUMER CREDIT

Consumer credit outstanding is an economic indicator which relates to
the ability of students and families to borrow additional funds to pay
for college.

The increases in consumer credit outstanding as a percent of disposable personal income to peak levels in the late 1980s after paydowns
during and after the recession of 1981–82 are shown on Chart A14.1.

STUDENT FINANCIAL AID

15. STUDENT FINANCIAL AID

Close to half of all students receive some form of student financial aid
to help pay for college. The availability of aid is a critical factor in en-
abling student to enroll in college.

Trends in student grants and loans are shown on Chart A15.1. Vir-

CHART A14.1. CONSUMER CREDIT OUTSTANDING AS A PERCENT OF DISPOSABLE PERSONAL INCOME

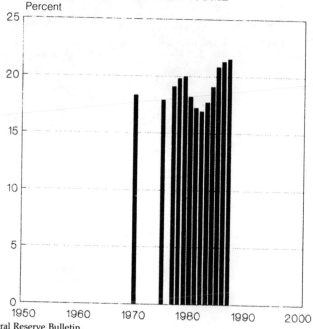

Percent

Source: Federal Reserve Bulletin.

CHART A15.1. FEDERAL STUDENT AID: CHANGING COMPOSITION FROM GRANTS TO LOANS

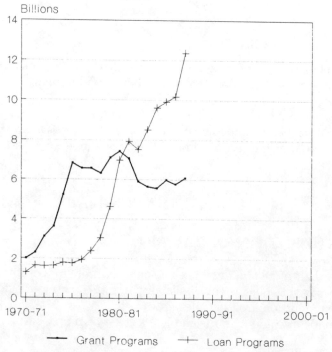

Billions

CHART A15.2. FEDERAL STUDENT AID: STUDENT GRANT PROGRAMS
(Current Dollars/Adjusted by Student Cost)

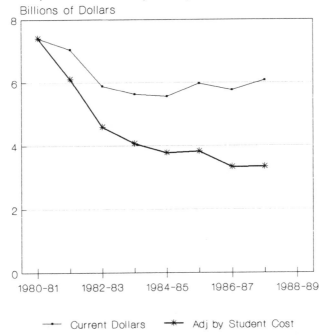

Billions of Dollars

— Current Dollars   —✱— Adj by Student Cost

CHART A16.1. EARNINGS INCREASE (Usual Weekly Earnings)

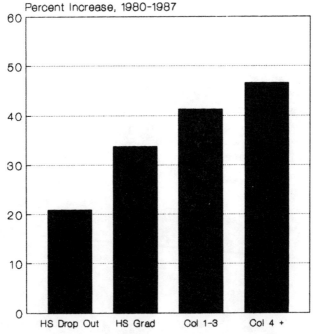

Percent Increase, 1980-1987

Source: U.S. Department of Labor.

tually all the growth of student aid in the 1980s has been in the form of loans.

The trends in student aid are trends in current dollars. To examine trends in the aid available to students, current dollars need to be adjusted for inflation. Typically, the Consumer Price Index has been used to adjust student aid for inflation, but the CPI does not reflect the education purchases that the students actually make. Using a mock-up of a student cost index and separating out grants—which reduce the cost of education—from loans—which do not—it appears that the real value of student grants at the end of the decade of the 1980s was not much more than half the value at the beginning of the decade. The trend in the value of student grants adjusting for inflation using a student cost index is shown on Chart A15.2.

EDUCATION OUTCOMES

16. RETURN ON INVESTMENT IN COLLEGE EDUCATION

Return on investment in college education is one economic indicator of educational outcomes that can influence demand for higher education.

The returns to investment in higher education have increased in recent years for two reasons. First, the entry-level jobs for young people with only a high school education are decreasing sharply, which increases the premium for a college education. Second, with the decline in the college-age population group, fewer young people are entering the labor force relative to the demand for educated workers, which is increasing their entering salaries.

One economic indicator to measure the trends in relative income of college-educated workers can be constructed using weekly earnings of college graduates compared with those of high school graduates.

DATA SOURCES

CHART A1.1. COLLEGE ENROLLMENTS

U.S. Department of Education, Office of Educational Research and Improvement, National Center for Education Statistics, *Digest of Education Statistics,* annual editions.

Updates of data not yet published can be obtained from the Information Service, Education Information Branch, at 1-800-424-1616.

The legislative history was obtained from committee reports of the U.S. Congress.

CHART A3.1. U.S. LABOR FORCE

U.S. Department of Labor, Bureau of Labor, Bureau of Labor Statistics, *Employment and Earnings,* April 1988, p. 7.

U.S. Department of Labor, Bureau of Labor Statistics, *Projections 2000,* Bulletin 2302 (March 1988), p. 92.

CHARTS A3.2, A3.3. CHANGES IN THE U.S. LABOR FORCE

U.S. Department of Labor, Bureau of Labor Statistics, Office of Employment Projections, *Monthly Labor Review,* November 1989.

CHART A3.4. EMPLOYMENT IN HIGHER EDUCATION

U.S. Department of Labor, Bureau of Labor Statistics, Office of Employment and Unemployment Statistics, Division of Occupational and Administrative Statistics.

CHART A4.1. INCREASES IN CURRENT FUND REVENUES

U.S. Department of Education, Office of Educational Research and Improvement, National Center for Education Statistics, *Digest of Education Statistics,* annual editions.

Updates of data not yet published can be obtained from the Information Service, Education Information Branch, at 1-800-424-1616.

CHART A4.4. STATE COLLEGE TUITION AND STATE COLLEGE APPROPRIATIONS

State Higher Education Executive Officers, Suite 310, 1860 Lincoln Street, Denver, Colorado 80295 (303-830-3685).

CHART A5.1. FEDERAL BUDGET DEFICIT

Council of Economic Advisors, *Economic Report of the President*, 1990, Table C-79, p. 387.

CHART A5.2. FEDERAL BUDGET ALLOCATIONS FOR NATIONAL PRIORITIES

Office of Management and Budget, Historical Tables.

CHART A5.3. FEDERAL BUDGET OUTLAYS, BY FUNCTION

Office of Management and Budget, Budget of the U.S. for FY 1990.

CHART A5.5. R&D FUNDING

National Science Foundation, *Academic Science and Engineering: R & D Funds*, Fiscal Year 1988, NSG 89-326.
Science and Engineering Indicators: 1989, NSB-89-1.

CHARTS A6.1, A6.2. VOLUNTARY SUPPORT FOR HIGHER EDUCATION

Council for Aid to Education, *Voluntary Support of Education*, annual editions.

Council for Aid to Education, 51 Madison Avenue, New York, New York 10010 (212-689-2400).

CHART A7.1. CORPORATE PROFITS

Council of Economic Advisors, *Economic Report of the President: 1990*, Table C-87, p. 395.

More recent data is compiled quarterly by the Bureau of Economic Analysis, Department of Commerce, and published in the *Survey of Current Business*.

CHART A8.1. COLLEGE ENDOWMENT

U.S. Department of Education, Office of Educational Research and Improvement, National Center for Education Statistics, *Digest of Education Statistics*, annual editions.

CHART A9.1. HIGHER EDUCATION PRICE INDEX

Higher Education Price Indexes: 1989 Update
Kent Halstead, Research Associates of Washington, 2605 Klingle
Road, N.W., Washington, D.C. 20008 (202-966-3326).

CHART A10.1. COLLEGE TUITION

U.S. Department of Education, Office of Educational Research and
Improvement, National Center for Education Statistics, *Digest of Education Statistics,* annual editions.

Consumer Price Index

U.S. Department of Commerce, *Survey of Current Business.* Recent
updates can be obtained from the U.S. Department of Labor, Bureau of Labor Statistics, 202-523-1239.

CHART A11.1. FACULTY SALARIES

American Association of University Professors, 1012 14th Street,
Washington, D.C. (202-737-5900).

CHART A11.2. REAL INCOME OF FACULTY

Calculated by Carol Frances + Associates (703-347-2365).

CHART A12.2. FAMILY/HOUSEHOLD INCOME

U.S. Department of Commerce, Bureau of the Census, *Current Population Reports,* Series P-60.

CHART A13.1. PERSONAL SAVINGS AS A PERCENT OF DISPOSABLE PERSONAL INCOME

Council of Economic Advisors, *Economic Report of the President,* 1990,
Table C-26, p. 324.

CHART A14.1. CONSUMER CREDIT

Council of Economic Advisors, *Economic Report of the President,* 1990,
Table C-75, p. 382.

CHART A15.1. STUDENT AID

The College Board, *Trends in Student Aid,* Annual editions.
The College Entrance Examination Board, 1717 Massachusetts Avenue, N.W., Washington, D.C. 20036 (202-332-7134).

CHART A15.2. STUDENT AID ADJUSTED BY STUDENT COST

Calculated by Carol Frances + Associates from College Board data.

CHART A16.1. EARNINGS INCREASE

Unpublished data obtained through the U.S. Department of Labor, Bureau of Labor Statistics, Office of Employment and Unemployment Statistics (202-523-1944).

INDEX